LiFe
WiTHOUT
ENVY

Also by
Camille DeAngelis

IMMACULATE HEART

BONES & ALL

MARY MODERN

PETTY MAGIC

ST. MARTIN'S GRIFFIN ⚄ NEW YORK

Ego Management
for Creative People

LiFe
WiTHOUT
ENVY

Camille
DeAngelis

www.stmartins.com

Designed by Anna Gorovoy

The Library of Congress Cataloging-in-Publication Data is available
upon request.

ISBN 978-1-250-09934-1 (trade paperback)
ISBN 978-1-250-09935-8 (e-book)

Our books may be purchased in bulk for promotional, educational,
or business use. Please contact your local bookseller or the Macmillan
Corporate and Premium Sales Department at 1-800-221-7945, extension
5442, or by e-mail at MacmillanSpecialMarkets@macmillan.com.

First Edition: September 2016

10   9   8   7   6   5   4   3   2   1

For my parents,
all three of them

CONTENTS

Introduction

Part I: Common Misapprehensions

Part II: Strategies and Inspiration

Introduction

A PINCHY SPOT

At the start of 2013 I was down to my last few hundred bucks. I hadn't done too badly with my first novel, but a corporate downsizing in 2010 left me with dreary prospects for the second, and after a lackluster publicity effort my publisher declined to issue the book in paperback. I went out of print at the age of thirty-one. A year or so later I set my comeback hopes on my first children's novel, but it didn't sell.

I was living at home with my mom. When I wasn't at my part-time job behind the customer service desk at the local Barnes & Noble, I was working on another novel in the "quiet room" at the library down the street. The writing was going well, but in my weaker moments I couldn't help feeling like things were *always* going to be like this: no more publisher, no "real" job, no home or family of my own. I didn't mind being single and childless, but I *did* care that my work hadn't received the recognition I felt it deserved.

Naturally, every time I logged onto Twitter or Facebook it seemed like someone else was announcing a book deal or a prestigious fellowship or a glowing newspaper review. I received a fellowship too—a monthlong writing retreat in a

Scottish castle!—but I felt ashamed that I had to borrow money from my mom for the airfare. It was a tremendously rewarding and productive month, but when I came home again I felt almost as stuck as I'd been before.

In the library where I'd go to write, people with whom I shared the "quiet room" would regularly answer phone calls as though they were in their own living rooms, or issue burps that registered on the Richter scale. I'd look up at this tacky red-and-purple quilt hanging on the wall and feel as though I were living inside an Ionesco play, unsure if I wanted to laugh or cry. I hated that spending my days in this public library made me feel so pissy and small.

Then it hit me:

It's the feeling trapped that's trapping me.

Rather like a Chinese finger puzzle, this realization changed everything—along with a little help from Eckhart Tolle.

THIS BOOK IS FOR YOU

When I ask people if they've heard of Eckhart Tolle and his books *The Power of Now* and *A New Earth*, I tend to get blank looks. It seems I run with a crowd who are *less* likely to read something if Oprah has recommended it. But there's a great deal of wisdom to be found on the self-help and New Age shelves, and it's a shame those labels turn so many people off. I'm a much happier and healthier artist for having read *The Power of Now*, and I'm writing this book to share what I've learned about the human ego with creatives like me who wouldn't otherwise encounter Tolle's work. "Every ego is a master of selective perception and distorted interpretation," he writes, and it seems to me that creative people—accustomed as we are to building whole worlds inside our heads!—are particularly susceptible to mistaking those distortions for reality. I see an urgent need for an open discussion about professional jealousy in the arts, both for our own mental wellness and for the benefit of our community.

If you're tired of comparing yourself to others, tired of feeling frustrated, anxious, undervalued, jealous,

invisible, inadequate, overlooked, taken advantage of, misunderstood: this book is for you.

(This book is for you even if you don't see yourself as an artist.)

A NASTY PLACE TO LIVE

The thing that qualifies me to write this little book is the same thing prompting you to read it. On the following page is a glimpse inside my brain when I'm in a pinchy spot.

superfluous shallow and self indulgent. *NOTHING I MAKE IS GOOD ENOUGH TO GET ME WHAT I WANT.* **It's true you know it is.** I am foolish and short sighted and petty and small. I am afraid that under my noble motives lay merely selfish ones, which is WORSE than just admitting I want millions of people to read my books and go on and on about how wonderful they are. Who the fuck do I think I am, anyway? How could I ever believe I have anything NEW and USEFUL to offer the world? There you go again, self indulgent and whiny. The world does not care. The world does not need ANOTHER WRITER. You are superfluous. Your "work" is frivolous. She has "the face of a slot." No one cares about what you have to offer. Think what I have to offer. No one will care if you do or don't care whether you will persist. All this poor-but-happy bohemian bullshit. WRINKLE DIE YOU DIE. This obsession with your work tells me how insecure you are. I'm tired of this, you're tired of this. I don't want to do this anymore. What is wrong with you? You are a privileged. You are really fucking ungrateful. Who do you think this is the world? I have art to the people the work is amazing something truly unprecedented. You are the same tired adjectives over and over. You're not saying anything anymore. Who do you think you are? You're small and petty and tiny and small. I don't write about things that really matter. I don't know what it feels like to really struggle against. I have never known hardship. I result isn't a sad and boring life essay. No wonder nobody gives a shit. Everything seems to tire me and it's all pointless. Ughhhhh. You act like you're humble but you're really actually full of yourself. **Is everyone else secretly as neurotic as I am or is it just me? Are you still neurotic even if you do a really good job of hiding it?** You're getting on everyone's nerves right now. You totally are, only they're too polite to let on. Story of your life. It isn't really, but that's the way you spin it, and you'll be stuck like that forever, bitter and small and always looking for the down side. You tell yourself this isn't who you are and then you

I will hazard a guess that on your bad days your mental ticker tape looks a lot like mine.

But is this how you want to live your life?

STRUGGLE IS OPTIONAL

First let's ruminate for a moment on the phrase "struggling writer." (If you are another kind of artist, just fill in your particular labels, hopes, and experiences over mine.)

At first you think: well, DUH, of course it's been a struggle! There have only ever been two choices, to struggle or to give up, and giving up is unthinkable. Therefore you struggle: to glue your butt to the chair, to come up with stories worth telling, to see the story through, to perform round after round of red-pen surgery, to find someone to believe in you, and then to find a team of bookworms tucked away in some Midtown skyscraper who'll believe in you too. Struggle and struggle and struggle some more. You can call it perseverance, but that's just struggle in a suit and tie.

And just when you think the struggle is over: blurbs, not enough blurbs, no blurbs, nightmares of a gaping black hole on the back cover. Prepub reviews. Spoilers. Snark. Marketing yourself. Social media blah blah blah. Sales figures. All the important newspapers that could have reviewed you, and didn't. A few faithful friends at your reading, asking you questions as if they don't know you just to make it look like you have a real audience. One- or two-star Amazon reviews (marked "helpful"—!) in which the reviewer can't even spell your name correctly. Envelopes you can't bring yourself to open because you know there's a royalty statement inside detailing how few books you've sold. Losing your editor. Losing your publisher. *Remainders.*

I used to think all of this "struggle" was inevitable. Every day I got to live in worlds I'd furnished myself, and I paid for that blessing with intermittent bouts of doubt and loathing (*maybe I'm a two-trick pony. Maybe I should pack it in and content myself with a steady paycheck*), not to mention some hilariously irrational jealousy (*why, why, WHY is EVERYBODY ON THE PLANET reading those COMPLETELY INANE VAMPIRE NOVELS?!?!*).

But I didn't *have* to live like this.

THE LAUGHTER OF SANITY

I went to India in April 2011, and in the course of my travels I met a girl who gave me a ride on the back of her motorbike. I was feeling frustrated about something, and told her about it. My new friend advised me to relax, to stop seeing petty inconveniences as capital-P problems. She told me that *The Power of Now* was changing her life. When I got home I picked up a copy, and "life-changing" actually seemed like an understatement.

Many years ago, when Eckhart Tolle was a student in London, he found himself on the Tube on his way to school one morning sitting opposite a woman who was talking agitatedly to herself. The train was crowded, but of course nobody wanted to sit anywhere near her. "And I said to her, who do you think you are?" the woman muttered. "How could you treat me this way? How could you betray my trust?" Tolle became interested. She was obviously mentally ill, but where was she headed? She was dressed like an ordinary commuter, but surely no one would hire a person in her condition!

The woman (still talking to herself) got off the train at Tolle's stop, and it turned out that she was studying or working in the very same building where Tolle was taking classes. He walked into the men's room and sidled up to the urinal, still pondering. *I hope I don't end up like that woman on the Tube,* he thought. Another man glanced up at him, hurriedly zipped up, and quit the restroom. Apparently Tolle had been thinking out loud. *Oh no!* he thought. *I'm already like her!*

Here's the thing: we are *all* talking to ourselves. The only difference between us "sane" people and that "crazy" woman is that she's doing it aloud. Tolle looked at himself in the mirror and began to laugh. To anyone else, he wrote, it would have sounded like the laughter of a madman—but it was truly "the laughter of sanity."

Tolle uses the woman on the train—replaying an argument with obsessive fervor—to exemplify the self-inflicted tragedy of our existence: we imprison ourselves in our minds. We enumerate our failures, sulking inside our heads like toddlers who didn't get their way. We take ourselves and our "problems" *so seriously.* The ego is an ugly, fragile little demon that gorges itself on our eternal discontent. Again and again we relive old traumas, bolster grudges, rehearse what we should have said, revel in our *rightness.* Nobody cares. Everyone treats us so unfairly. We measure ourselves against the achievements and the smiling, shiny exteriors of others, and we always, *always* fall short. Basically, life is shit.

Except that it isn't. Like a ritual that works because you believe it will, a problem becomes a problem when you label it as such. A struggle, by definition, perpetuates itself. This isn't just semantics. When that quiet, unflappable part of you—the you beyond your ego—detaches itself from the endless stream of mental bullshit and listens to it as it flows by (not judging, just listening), suddenly something begins to shift. The simple act of observing the voice proves that you are not the source of it.

There has been nothing more empowering than the realization that I don't have to think thoughts that bring me pain.

—DR. JILL BOLTE TAYLOR

A CASE IN POINT

Now you may be thinking, *It'd be AWESOME if I could stop believing my negative ticker tape. I really want to be a happier person. But where do I even start?*

I'll begin with a concrete example. One morning—right in the middle of that pinchy spot I told you about earlier—I picked up the arts section of *The Philadelphia Inquirer* and found a front-page, above-the-fold feature on a debut novelist. Here is pretty much exactly what ran through my head:

> *What the f**k? I'm way more local than this guy, and the* Inquirer *book editors completely ignored both my novels. Uh-huh, a bildungsroman. Big deal. And they're sending this guy on a twenty-city book tour? WHAT THE F**K?*

Ordinarily this sort of thing would have thrown me into a funk for the rest of the day. But this time I was determined to respond to my thoughts in a different way. I thought to myself, *So that's what it means to be stuck inside my head!* A marvelous calm settled over me as I refolded the newspaper and laid it on the table. *This isn't me. It may be baggage, but I can let go of it anytime.* And I did. I walked to the library and got back to my world building.

There are plenty more examples where this came from. Yeah, I do still have those internal tantrums sometimes, but now part of me is able to wade out from the stream of mental sludge and watch it as it passes, smiling at the madness. I recognize what the psychologist Timothy D. Wilson calls "repetitive, circular rumination," and I gently disengage from it, again and again (and again).

Let me emphasize that *anyone* can make this shift.

(Yes, even you.)

WHAT IS EGO, ANYWAY?

You probably know that the word "ego" comes from the Latin *ego*, meaning "I." According to the *Online Etymology Dictionary*, "ego" in its eighteenth-century metaphysical usage refers to "the self: that which feels, acts, or thinks," and "ego" in the sense of "conceit" didn't come into play until 1891.

The second entry is perhaps even more germane to our purposes. "Egoism," a metaphysical term dating to 1785, is "the theory that a person has no proof that anything exists outside his own mind."

At the dawn of human life you needed to feel that, against all odds, your life was worth preserving. Freudian distinctions aside, your ego *was* your survival instinct.

A million years later, you are no longer that hairy ape loping on hind limbs across the savannah. Your concerns are way less primal now. Compared to your distant ancestors, you may as well be an earl in an English manor house—so genteel that human emotions need never be discussed, let alone felt. You ride purebred horses down the country back lanes, passing rainy afternoons in your library of thousands of leather-bound first editions. You use words like "ascot" and "aperitif" without irony or humor.

And your ego? He's the servant who simpers out of fear for his position, managing to convince you that you are incapable of fixing your own sandwich. He riles you up with that panicky feeling of can't-get-along-without-it, take-it-or-someone-else-will even though you no longer need that instinct to survive. But not even the least evolved part of your personality wants to hear you've outgrown it, so the ego keeps trucking along filling you with doubts and fears and all the while thinking it's doing you a favor.

THREE VIGNETTES
ON THE NATURE OF THE EGO

1.

A pop star tweets about another musician twenty years her senior, who had confessed to someone else that she wasn't really a fan of the younger artist's music. "When artists grow old and begin to recognize their own mortality they throw shade at younger spirits," she writes. "We see it happen ALL the time. Whether or not you like me . . . you are WATCHING, and that's what's most important . . . People are seriously intimidated by my talent and honesty."

One wonders if she'll react with any more humility when, twenty years from now, some glitter-dusted upstart says something to the same effect about *her*.

2.

(There are three egos in this one. See if you can spot them.)

Not so long ago I went on a date with a man I'd met in a coffee shop. He drove me to a secondhand bookstore and café in an old mill overlooking a river and we went inside and started browsing the tables. I picked up a certain book of nonfiction, the title of which has no bearing on this story. "Hey," I said to my date. "Didn't this guy get nailed for plagiarism?"

"There's no such thing as plagiarism," said a man browsing across the table from us. I hadn't noticed him until he inserted himself into our conversation. "I'm a published writer myself, so I can tell you that people may talk about stealing other people's ideas, but there's really nothing new or original out there."

Having been falsely accused of plagiarism myself, there was no way I was going to let this slide. "Actually, there *is* such a thing as plagiarism," I said. "You take someone else's words, *word for word,* and pass them off as your own. That is plagiarism."

The man continued speaking as if he hadn't heard me, and I felt my date stiffen with anticipation. "Well, *I'm* a published author too," he cut in, "and *I* think . . ."

I assumed what I believed to be a dignified silence, waiting for both of them to stop talking before I suggested my date and I go upstairs for lunch.

Why did I feel compelled to correct that man? Why did each of them need to have the last word in a pointless debate with a perfect stranger? And why did I walk away thinking, *I am so above this*?

3.

But before I met that guy, I met another guy. I'd chatted with him at a picnic and he e-mailed me a couple days later about getting together for coffee. I liked him, I thought he was a really lovely man, but for some reason I kept waffling about setting a date for that drink.

Still, I mentioned him when my sister asked for an update on my love life.

"Why don't you go out with him?" she asked.

I shrugged. "I don't know. I just can't get excited enough to bother making plans."

She answered me lightheartedly, but she was joking on the square: "Why don't you want to be happy?"

You're probably wondering what this last one has to do with my ego. I mention it because that line, *Why don't you want to be happy?*, slices to the very heart of how the ego functions.

If you are happy without it, then by definition you don't *need* it. It has long since outgrown its primordial usefulness, but the ego won't give itself up that easily.

Sometimes it's petulant and sometimes it's self-righteous. It can play the victim or go on the attack. Sometimes it swears you're amazing, incredible, *the best,* and other times it declares you'll never amount to anything no matter *how* hard you work. However it operates, you've got to train yourself not to believe what your ego tells you about who you are, what you're capable of, and what you "deserve." Your sanity is at stake.

You may very well be addicted to your thoughts. The ego is insatiable, after all. So you must approach this problem the way you would any other addiction: determine a course of detoxification—to confront and resolve your shadow self, as Jung would say—and adhere to it even when things get squirmy, as they inevitably will.

Reading this book is a good place to start. First we'll run through some common beliefs and assumptions that keep us dissatisfied with our lives and work, and then we'll explore some enjoyable ways to go about systematically un-believing them. **Make a sincere effort to examine your own ego, delving into uncomfortable emotions with honesty and compassion, and you *will* find it in you to be happy— *lastingly* happy—no matter how your career is (or isn't) going, and regardless of anyone else's achievements or opinions.**

Whether or not you're a writer, you'll want to keep a notebook to jot down your reactions and insights as they arise. **This growth process is way too important not to make a record of it.**

PART I

*Common
Misapprehensions*

Let's make sure our ideas of success are our own,
that we are truly the authors of our own ambitions.

—ALAIN DE BOTTON

PERSONAL AGENCY?
YOU'D LIKE TO THINK SO!

Misapprehension #1: *My thoughts are entirely my own. The way I think about the world, and my place in it, is completely unique to me.*

CAPITALISTS DESIGNED THE AMERICAN PUBLIC EDUCATION SYSTEM TO TURN CHILDREN INTO OBEDIENT WORKERS.

I know this sounds like the musings of a conspiracy theorist, but let's examine the facts: in 1843 US Congressman Horace Mann traveled to Prussia, where this civic-minded educational system was already in place, and when he got back to America he lobbied to emulate it. Educational historians laud Horace Mann as the champion of free public schooling to help children grow into educated voters, but there is a dark side to this system: his efforts opened classrooms to those kids *besides* boys from wealthy families, but in doing so Mann advocated for an orderly society at the expense of the individual. His educational vision implied that the "common" child—one not born into privilege—should learn to follow rules and directions rather than inventing his own, and for that Mann is remembered as the "Father of the Common School." It is not much of a generalization to say that in a traditional school environment, conformity is valued over innovation. Sir Ken Robinson makes this argument in his 2006 TED Talk, "Do Schools Kill Creativity?," and it's the most-watched TED video of all time because we know how right he is.

When you actually stop to consider it—which probably isn't often—you can see how we are brought up to be good little workers, good little consumers. How many of your childhood desires—for toys, pets, junk food, Halloween costumes—were influenced by advertisements and commercials? Did you ever ask a parent or teacher why something was done in a particular way, only to be shut down with a variation of "because I said so"? How many times did the hunger for approval win out over curiosity and imagination?

You might begin to suspect that even your most cherished and private ambitions are double agents in the service of that destiny. It makes sense, right? We are made to feel that we must always be striving for more. A bigger house, more money, more success, because if you feel complete just as you are, then you're no longer a cog in the system. You are insuggestible and therefore unprofitable. Corporations need you to feel inadequate. They need you to *want all the things*. They're selling you an idea of individuality that they've created, and selling you the products that will keep you believing in this illusion. It's in their interest to let you think you have personal agency, that you're making all your own decisions. There's a reason why *The Matrix* was such a successful movie.

Train yourself to think more critically about what you truly believe and want, what actually makes you happy. What are your favorite foods? Your favorite films and music? What did you want to be when you grew up and why, and how did you come to do what you're doing now? What appeals to you and what disgusts you, and *why*? If you keep looking you'll begin to see your biases and your assumptions, and how you came to hold them in the first place.

If you think that as a creative individual you are above all this shallow materialism and mindless conformity, that it doesn't apply to you, think again. Artists have their own carnival of bullshit to contend with, and it might be even more insidious. We've convinced ourselves we're striving not for our own glory but for the benefit of art, of literature, of culture, but we still "need" the MacBook Pro to write our screenplay. We "need" the diploma from a "prestigious" school if we wish to be taken seriously in our chosen field. We "need" the top-of-the-line art supplies and music equipment and lessons with the most respected teacher in our echelon. I'm not saying we can't legitimately benefit from these resources—just that we shouldn't identify with the trappings.

If you want to slough off this culturally imposed bullshit, you have to go and sit in a very quiet place where no one can possibly interrupt you. Ask yourself, "How much of this is actually mine?"

Do you even want what you think you want?

*Don't let anyone tell you, ever, that this is a
zero-sum game. Your genius does not threaten me.
It delights and inspires me.*

—SEANAN McGUIRE

SWEET LITTLE BLOBS
OF TEMPORARY PERSONHOOD

Misapprehension #2: *We are isolated and competitive individuals, forever jostling with strangers for a seat on the bus at the end of a long day.*

In fourth grade I got to duck out of some of the regular subjects each week to attend "Challenge" classes. Only two students in the whole grade could say they were in "Challenge Everything"—literature, math, art, *and* music—and I was one of them. You can tell by the way I'm recounting this that I was a bit too proud of it. A classmate, who would become one of the stars on the high school basketball team, once told me (half wistfully, half resentfully) that if there were only a "Challenge Gym," well then, *he'd* be in it. Looking back on it now, I understand why that kid didn't like me.

As children we are told that no two snowflakes are precisely alike, that each of us is "special" and "unique," but even when we are small we can sniff the poop under the platitude. We may be too young yet to articulate this, but we understand on an instinctive level that if everyone is *special*—if every watercolor in the middle school art show gets a ribbon—then there's no real value to the word. So, through the preferential treatment of our parents and teachers, we come to believe that some of us are more special than others: more talented, more fortunate, and therefore more deserving of success later on in life.

Did I just say "more deserving"? Shouldn't I have said "better equipped"?

The competitive spirit of American capitalism gave us the Prius and the iPhone, but it also fosters a sense of insecurity from which none of us are immune. Only some of us can win approval; only a few of us will become rich and famous. In our classrooms and on the nightly news (along with what's deemed not "important" enough to make the news) we are implicitly taught, as Noam Chomsky says, that some of us matter and some of us don't.

And yet we all know, despite this conditioning, that my life is no more valuable than that of a thirty-four-year-old woman living in abject poverty on the far side of the world. So we have to throw out these bullshit conceptions of uniqueness and chosenness if we want to talk about the nature of my identity in relation to yours.

Let's reflect for a moment on the parameters of your identity, shall we?

Your name.

Your face.

Your parents.

Your ethnicity.

Your socioeconomic background.

Your abilities and disabilities.

You didn't choose any of this, though, did you?

The Illusion of Separation

The "oneness" concept appears time and again across the spectrum of religious and philosophical traditions, though we may put different language around it. This principle is most prominent in the Hindu and Buddhist traditions, but we catch the occasional glimpse of it within the Abrahamic belief systems as well. It's the unity of all created things, the notion that "God"—or however you'd prefer to name the intelligence that created us—separated itself into seemingly discrete parts so that it might come to know itself, and that this separation, *your ego,* is entirely illusory. The Hindu tradition has a beautiful word, *maya,* for the power used by gods and demons alike to produce these illusions, and another, *lila,* which means "divine play." If the gods are making us dance simply to amuse themselves, well then, we might as well relax and enjoy the party.

It brings me a continual sense of peace to think of myself as a sweet little blob of temporary personhood. What if we all really do come out of a cosmic Play-Doh container? What if we're all made of the same stuff molded into different shapes?

So you see, you're *not* special. And that is the one great and profound benediction underwriting your entire existence.

your third—grade teacher

that kid
who played
Chunk in
The Goonies

you

me

This may seem like New Age nonsense at first, but hear me out. I believe you can fairly judge every philosophy by its effect once you've spent a bit of time testing it. *Does this help my life work better?* Yes or no, the answer is generally pretty clear. Consider these lines from the *Brihadaranyaka Upanishad*:

> *He was afraid; therefore one who is all alone is afraid. He reflected, "Since there is nothing other than me, of what am I afraid?" Then his fear vanished, for of what could he have been afraid?*

If we're all created out of a single source, then you come from the same place as everything you're afraid of. The Hindu philosophers are telling us that, spiritually speaking, there is no monster lurking under the bed. Yes, there are stock market crashes and lethal diseases and occasionally pieces of exploded airplane fall out of the sky. And it's true that there are people in the world who would do you physical harm given half an opportunity. But there are also people in this world who make peace with their terminal diseases and forgive their attackers, because they are able to recognize that there is so much more to this than *this*.

We have to allow for what the psychologist Eric Maisel calls "necessary arrogance"—no art ever comes into being without the artist's belief that she has a worthwhile contribution to make—but don't let your ego talk you into taking that contribution too seriously. When you subscribe to the theory of oneness, you feel buoyed by other people's good fortune and success instead of threatened or diminished by it. It's much easier to feel happy when good things happen to good people, and much more natural to empathize when horrible things happen to good people.

Best of all, when good things happen to *you*, you get to share your joy instead of hoarding it—which is, of course, a self-enhancing cycle: your attitude and emotions giving you ever more reason to feel what you're already feeling.

Any sufficiently advanced technology is indistinguishable from magic.

—ARTHUR C. CLARKE

FUTURE SCIENCE

Misapprehension #3: *I know myself. I know what I am capable of. I know my limits.*

When I go to Edinburgh I like to haunt the mezzanine of the main reading room at the National Library of Scotland. On my first trip a few years ago I indulged a fascination with *Borderland,* a quarterly journal of psychical research published between 1893 and 1897 by W. T. Stead, who later died on the *Titanic.* Much of the material in this short-lived magazine is sensationalist if not downright hokey, but I still found quite a few articles worth the ink they were printed with. The most remarkable concerned the autopsy of a blind man. The doctor found gray matter—brain cells!—inside the cadaver's fingertips. The blind man quite literally thought with his fingers.

It's often said that any phenomenon with a whiff of magic about it is something we *will* be able to study empirically in the future. Science simply hasn't caught up yet. This seems like the only sensible way to regard all that we don't yet understand: to *admit* that we don't understand it.

The blind man's autopsy—along with plenty of other weird

phenomena studied by the more flexibly minded among the scientific community—hint that consciousness is *not* housed inside the brain, that it is not localized at all. (Take for another example the neurons in our navel region, providing for that oh-so-reliable "gut feeling.") Max Planck, winner of the Nobel Prize in physics in 1918 and the father of quantum theory, would not have pooh-poohed the work of psychical researchers. "I regard consciousness as fundamental," he declared in 1931. "I regard matter as derivative from consciousness. We cannot get behind consciousness. Everything that we talk about, everything that we regard as existing, postulates consciousness." It isn't brain matter that enables consciousness, Planck is saying—it's the other way around.

Scientists can't measure the percentage of our neurological activity occurring on the conscious level—UC Santa Barbara neuroscientist Michael Gazzaniga believes it's roughly 2 percent—but this means we *can* say that something like 98 percent of our mental processes are happening subliminally. In other words: you are a mystery to yourself. You have *no idea* what you are capable of.

It's a terrifying thought, but kind of sexy too, right? *You aren't even aware of your own secrets.*

You can actually use the fact that you don't know most of what's going on in your own mind to your creative advantage. This book is the perfect example: in 2011 and 2012 I kept a notebook with copious scribblings on anything that tickled my interest: the shared dreams of the Sufi mystics; the very best lines from *Doctor Who* or *The Power of Myth*, Joseph Campbell's interviews with Bill Moyers. It felt important that I should read and make notes on anything I felt drawn to, anything at all, even though I didn't have any idea what I was working toward. I'd purchased the notebook at a stationery shop in Florence in 2002; the cover is made from heavy paper with images from a medieval tarot, and it has graph-paper pages. This Florentine notebook has a ritual air about it, so much so that it took me ten years to get to the last page. I saved it for the good stuff.

When I pulled this notebook off the shelf recently I was stunned to see how thoroughly I'd laid the foundations for *Life Without Envy*. It was like drawing a map of an imaginary place and then traveling to find it, exactly as I'd designed it, there and navigable in real life. A piece of me, another tendril of my consciousness, was already here.

So you make space in the parlor that is your conscious mind, knowing that it is only one room in the house where your soul lives. You put the kettle on, waiting for the knock at the front door but not at all surprised to hear the footfalls on the stair. You follow your curiosity wherever it leads you, even into the darkest, filthiest crawl spaces. You remember that you *don't* know, that you *don't* have a clue, and when the magic announces itself you'll know just what to call it.

There is here no measuring with time, no year matters, and ten years are nothing. Being an artist means, not reckoning and counting, but ripening like the tree which does not force its sap and stands confident in the storms of spring without the fear that after them may come no summer.

—RAINER MARIA RILKE

HURRY UP AND BE
SOMEBODY

Misapprehension #4: *I just need to prove myself as soon as possible, and then I'll be someone important.*

During my freshman year at NYU I took the subway uptown to the Guggenheim. When I came upon Picasso's *Le Moulin de la Galette*—painted just after the renowned artist's nineteenth birthday—I stood before it in a fog of self-reproach. *I* was nineteen, and what did I have to show for myself?

In that moment I succumbed to "wunderkind syndrome": the frantic desire to produce an amazing work of art as soon as possible so that everyone will hail your genius before any of your contemporaries can edge you out. Furthermore, if you're not applying yourself to this ambition with all-consuming focus then you obviously don't want it badly enough, and if you don't want it enough to give up sleep, social life, and basic personal hygiene, then you musn't be a *true* artist.

Ridiculous, right? Why do we want so badly to prove our brilliance at a more tender age than everyone else? Why, in our secret (or not-so-secret) hearts, do we want to be perceived as *better* than everyone else?

Perhaps the first reason is, of course, that our culture is obsessed with youth, and generally at the expense of substance. We feel this panic to produce something while the world still casts us in an attractive light. This pressure is especially acute for those of us working in the performing arts; one of my roommates at NYU, a dancer, would receive her degree in three years instead of four to put her on the full-time hamster wheel of auditions and callbacks as soon as possible.

The second factor to consider is the scarcity mentality, which has haunted our species from that African savannah all the way to the Walmart Black Friday stampede. There are only so many accolades to go around—only so much gallery space, only so many roles in the show, only so many slots on the "big five" publishers' seasonal lists—and we grow desperate to claim our share as soon as we can.

But the ultimate reason has nothing to do with cutting throats or getting trampled. We all want to be loved and accepted for who we are, and because our art feels like the truest expression of that identity, it's all too tempting to conflate output with intrinsic worth. This misperception is most powerful during that brutal passage through adolescence. *I must beam this work of my heart out into the world so that I will be seen—heard—understood.* If we must make ourselves vulnerable in this way, then we might as well be rewarded for our bravery.

When I first began writing fiction with an eye toward publication, in 2001, a nineteen-year-old with a book deal was quite unusual. These days, thanks to the rocketing popularity of young adult fiction and the ease of digital publishing, you can find teenaged authors seemingly everywhere you look. One of these authors, whose self-publishing success led to a million-dollar deal with a big five publisher, has mentioned in interviews that she wanted to publish by the age of twenty-six because that's how old Stephen King was when he came out with his first novel.

I know where she was coming from. Just before my twenty-second birthday, I finished the last scene of a six-hundred-page manuscript, hit the print button, and mailed that teetering pile of paper off to a literary agent. I look back on the girl I was then and try not to smile too condescendingly: it was unprofessional to be sending a first draft to literary agents and naïve at best to expect an offer from a major publisher only a couple of months down the line. Eventually I figured this out, and wound up putting the years before my first book deal to good use: writing all night, sleeping 'til noon, forging lasting friendships with my grad school classmates, and going to classes knowing only that I had a hell of a lot to learn. In essence, I was working on a much more practical form of character development: I stopped believing the world owed me something and focused on telling an engaging and meaningful story.

In *Show Your Work!* Austin Kleon cites John Richardson's

biography of Picasso. According to Richardson, Picasso was notorious for sucking the creative vitality out of anyone who paid him a visit: somebody with stars in his eyes would show up hoping to be inspired by the great artist, only to leave hours later feeling nervous, exhausted, and depressed. "Picasso had made off with their energy and would go off to his studio and spend all night living off it," Richardson wrote. The sculptor Constantin Brancusi called him a cannibal and a vampire, and he wasn't the only one of Picasso's contemporaries who wanted nothing to do with him personally.

It's the most natural thing in the world for artists to congregate and exchange energy and ideas, but the man who created that painting at the Guggenheim I so envied was all take and no give. He acted as if these hopeful, naïve artists knocking on his door *did* owe him something.

The asshole-genius is a false binary—you can see a canvas you painted at age nineteen in one of the world's most prestigious art museums without turning into a psychic vampire—but we may still find ourselves striving for notoriety at any cost if we lose sight of these two basic truths:

1. Getting a book, film, or record deal does NOT make you a better artist. (Indeed, it does not make you any more of an artist than you were before.)

2. Getting a book, film, or record deal does NOT make you a better person.

In his 2008 TED Talk, Benjamin Zander, the conductor of the Boston Philharmonic Orchestra, said, "I have a definition of success. For me, it's very simple: it's not about wealth and fame and power. It's about how many shining eyes I have around me."

Zander is now in his seventies, and one gets the distinct impression as he bounds down the steps to engage with his audience that he is sharing the wisdom he has accumulated over seven decades of conscious living. He has nothing to prove; he's only offering the best that is in him, a trove of abundance that goes on accumulating with every passing year.

How absurd, then, to think that one's insight and ability have a sell-by date, as if we artists spoil like yogurt instead of maturing like wine. Art isn't a sporting event. No one is standing before you with a stopwatch. Besides, there's always going to be someone out there who's achieved *your* goal at a younger age, who's garnered more commercial success or critical accolades and awards. Wunderkind syndrome will siphon off your creative energy if you give in to it; don't doubt it's possible to be the vampire *and* the victim.

But the even more critical point is this: you are worthy of love and esteem regardless of what you paint or fail to paint, what you write or never get around to writing, what you share or what you keep to yourself. If you believe you need to earn love and esteem, you can strive and suffer for approval but what you receive will not actually be love. You have to trust in your own right to be here before anyone else can agree with you.

There is nothing noble in being superior to your fellow man; true nobility is being superior to your former self.

—ERNEST HEMINGWAY (ATTRIBUTED)

ANOTHER PERNICIOUS FANTASY

Misapprehension #5: *I mean it, though. If I can't be the best, then I don't deserve to be here.*

There's something else Eckhart Tolle says that has stuck with me, and I suspect it will do you good to hear it too.

> *"Greatness" is a mental abstraction and a favorite fantasy of the ego.*

This line makes me giddy every time I read it. If it doesn't ultimately matter how impressed other people are (or aren't) with our efforts, then what's left is absolute creative freedom. *You mean I can just chill out and enjoy the storytelling for my own satisfaction?*

"Greatness"—as we typically interpret it in this twisted, vapid culture of ours—is an illusion. We're forever confusing recognition with inherent value. If Leonardo had been preoccupied with painting a *Last Supper* scene that would "last through the ages," he wouldn't have experimented with that weird mixture of oil and tempera on dry plaster. But he took that risk, got *on* with it, and made something the monks of Santa Maria delle Grazie would appreciate every time they sat down to eat.

The concepts of "greatness" and "mediocrity" are pernicious fantasies. Eradicate these words from your mind as if they were a virus, because in a sense, they are.

First let's consider the logical absurdity. "Who's in charge of measuring everyone else's achievements?" the psychologist Ellen Langer has asked. "Who made that yardstick?" Even if you can answer this rhetorical question—your mother, the executive at the record label, your high school art teacher who thought she was doing you a favor by saying, "You don't have it in you to be the kind of artist you want to be"—you have to admit that you are giving these people power and influence they do not intrinsically possess.

This isn't about comparing your career to someone else's, coming up short, and feeling shitty about it. This pernicious fantasy affects us on the inside, tainting our personal lives, and our personal lives are our bedrock. The underlying issue here isn't *mediocrity*. It's a lack of humility. It's so tempting to dismiss my high school classmates who've gone the route of kids, mortgage, and 9-to-5 office jobs as "mediocre," and I'd be lying if I said I've never given in to it. When we talk about wanting to be "great," we implicitly set ourselves above others. We see ourselves as *chosen* where others are not. And is there anything remotely honorable about narcissism?

I've recently been introduced to a new way of looking at the words *ordinary* and *extraordinary*. In this worldview—articulated by the philologist Franklin Edgerton by way of my Hinduism professor—an *ordinary* life is an *unexamined* life. In this paradigm, the plumber who watches *The Power of Myth* and discusses it with his wife over homemade pizza on a Saturday night is indeed living an extraordinary life, a life of questioning and delving for hidden meaning, of seeking (and finding) spiritual succor in even the most unlikely places. In this sense, true "greatness"—if we must use that word—lies in simply using what we've been given, of pushing our frontiers and redrawing our own borders. If I'm right—if human achievement lies in what I like to call "manifesting the awesome" rather than tapping one's inherent ability—then we *all* have the capacity for "genius," even those whom traditional science and medicine have labeled abnormal or inadequate in some way. In this paradigm, mediocrity is a habit rather than a life sentence.

When I was very young I wanted to be a "great" novelist, but now I just think in terms of the next project, of how it will stretch and frighten me. If I draw a comparison, I measure who I am against who I could be, the person I can grow into if I remain willing, over a period of years, to stick out my neck day after day. If I don't illustrate my own stories, if I don't write with candor about my feelings of jealousy and inadequacy, if I don't someday stand up in front of a thousand people and speak articulately (despite my thundering heart) about all these topics of such critical importance to all of us—ego and humility and creativity and intuition—then I will have to look back on my career and acknowledge that it has been a mediocre one. This judgment will have nothing to do with anyone else's standards or opinions, and everything to do with my own.

Jim was like a sailor who had studied the compass and found that there was a fifth dimension in which one could sail.

—JERRY JUHL ON JIM HENSON

MANIFESTING THE AWESOME

Misapprehension #6: *My ideas belong to me.*

Call to mind the greatest creative achievement of your life so far. It might be a poem, or a painting, or a Web site design. An invention. A libretto. A starring role. This is the endeavor you are most proud of.

Whatever it is, gather all the memories you have of making it, and recall your various feelings as you worked, all the ecstatic moments as well as the moments of frustration. Recall your secret hopes for this project too—did you dream of publishing it, exhibiting it, performing it in front of a rapt audience of thousands? Did you hope it would be so completely realized, and so well received, that your father would finally, *finally* tell you he is proud of you?

Now, with all this in mind, read the following lines and pay attention to your physical reaction.

This work of art is not "yours."

You don't own it. It doesn't belong to you.

You are not the origin of this work.

Now you might be feeling a little indignant, right? *All that work, and it isn't MINE?*

Or perhaps you see where I might be going with this. Maybe you're already familiar with Carl Jung's theory of the collective unconscious—that cosmic stew of memory and experience to which we all have access—although that isn't exactly what I'm getting at. Twenty-four centuries ago Plato talked about how ideas are basically free agents hanging out in the ether, and that sometimes (if we're lucky) they tap us on the shoulder. While it's up to us to see them through, they still don't belong to anyone in particular.

I have published four books so far, and mundanely speaking, of course it *is* my work. But when the writing is going smoothly and I feel exhilarated by the creative process—when I'm in "theta state" or "the zone" or whatever you want to call it—I understand that I am tapping an infinite reservoir, kind of like going to the beach with an orange plastic bucket and dipping it into the surf. Now, is that "my" cupful of ocean?

This is what I mean by "manifesting the awesome." Good ideas don't originate in my brain—they come *through* me. I write them down and eventually share them. I no longer try to possess them. I no longer identify with them. My name goes on the book cover because I need food and a roof over my head.

Sure, I have to relinquish my pride, that sense of owner-ship—what the Hindu tradition calls *ahankara,* or "mine-ness"—

but there's something even more satisfying in the feeling of connection you get when you become an amanuensis as opposed to a solitary "genius." For a little while I get to be reabsorbed into the beautiful thing I came out of, the beautiful thing that made me. (And if you have a hard time slipping into the elusive "theta state"—that relaxed, dreamy, ultracreative brain mode—Plato's concept of ideas might be the credo that opens your way in.)

You can try this on a provisional basis, right? Just step into it in the spirit of *what-if,* and see how you feel. I bet you'll find that when you release your claim to the work, you'll see how it frees you to embrace whatever's coming next.

THE CONSOLATION

Blest is the maid, and truly blest alone,
Who peaceful lives, unknowing and unknown.
For her the world displays no winning charms;
No love of conquest her fair bosom warms;
Within her breast no warring passion glows;
No anxious wish disturbs her fix'd repose;
No faithless lover fills her eyes with tears;
No haughty rival's fatal charms she fears;
No love neglected sinks her soul with shame;
She secret mourns no ill-requited flame.
Unmindful of her charms, however fair,
Unknown the pride of beauty, or the care;
Hid from the world, she shuns the public eye,
Like roses, that in deserts bloom and die.
In peace and ease she spends her happy days,
And fears no envy, as she courts no praise.

—ELIZABETH SCOT (1729-1789)

FEAR NO ENVY,
COURT NO PRAISE

Misapprehension #7: *I'm not a "real" artist until I make my work public.*

At the beginning of 2013 I spent a glorious four-week residency at Hawthornden Castle, which is situated on a sandstone cliff overlooking a curve of the River North Esk, six or eight miles outside Edinburgh in Scotland. I'd hoped to sink into a new novel, a fantasy set in eighteenth-century Edinburgh, but just before my departure my agent asked for a substantial revision of a novel I'd prematurely washed my hands of. I still managed a bit of research reading for the new project, however, and that's how I discovered the Enlightenment-era poet Elizabeth Scot.

Scot, formerly Miss Rutherford, began writing poetry after her first fiancé was lost at sea. Robert Burns had admiring words for her work at the time, and while Scotland's most revered poet certainly had a reputation with the milkmaids, his seductive ways would not have extended as far as his evaluation of a lady's literary capabilities; Burns regarded Elizabeth

Scot as a true poet. But in Scot's day, women writers generally circulated their manuscripts among their friends, leaving the risks and rewards of publication to their male counterparts. Her poem "The Consolation" reflects the prevailing opinion of the day: to seek any sort of notoriety for one's efforts was *unseemly*.

Needless to say, this revelation chafed at my twenty-first-century feminist sensibility. The notion of writing something with no intention of sending it out into the wider world was inconceivable to me. Granted, as the wife of a "country gentleman of considerable property" there was no need for Scot to seek a living, as I do, but when I first tried to imagine myself in her place I actually felt a spasm of panic.

The more I sat with "The Consolation," though, the more comfortable I became with Elizabeth's way of showing her work. Were my modern priorities any more sensible or fulfilling? I had chosen a path that would reduce the value of my work to a "P&L," the "profit and loss" sheet a publisher draws up to decide whether or not you're worth the advance money. Anonymous reviewers and commenters snarked at my plot, my characters, even the youthful nervous enthusiasm I displayed in a national radio interview. My first publisher gave up on me before my second novel even came out. But most of all, I was tired of pretending not to care how my stories were received. I began to see a weird sort of freedom in that obsolete practice of manuscript circulation; I wanted some of that eighteenth-century womanly equanimity for myself.

Looking back, I see I met Elizabeth Scot at just the right time. I'll go on publishing my work—seeing as no one else is going to feed and clothe me—but if my next book bombs I'll waste neither breath nor ink likening it to a rose wilting in the desert sun. You have no say over the century into which you're born, or inhospitable climates; so why not give of the best that's in you, and move on?

[I]t is worth wondering what the need to be special prevents us seeing about ourselves—other, that is, than the unfailing transience of our lives; what the need to be special stops us from being.

—ADAM PHILLIPS

THE CORPSE IN THE ATTIC

Misapprehension #8: *I must make sacrifices for my art.*

The summer I was nine, my dad dropped me off for my first day of camp. No one had informed him that a field trip was on the calendar for this particular day (I was coming in mid-program), and that lunch would not be provided. I wound up at the Renaissance Faire without two nickels to clink together, and we were there *all day*. I remember looking up at a lemonade stand with almost unbearable longing, envying every child who walked away from that counter with a tall plastic cup rattling with ice cubes.

I couldn't enjoy the wacky medieval costumes or the archery or the make-believe jousting. I was too effing thirsty.

Looking back on that day, I find it incredible that none of the camp counselors seemed to notice or care about my predicament. My dad was thoroughly guilt stricken when he found out that night, even though it wasn't his fault. Why hadn't I simply asked someone to loan me a couple dollars?

This may sound like just another unfortunate footnote in the story of a childhood, but I often wonder if I internalized something unproductive that day. Even at the age of nine I believed that not asking for help proved my resilience, that preserving my pride was more important than eating when I was hungry.

In the years between then and now I have often caught myself thinking in terms of "not enough." I have been that girlfriend feeling neglected when her guy wanted to socialize with new acquaintances at a party. I have been that writer trying to stretch one advance check over two calendar years. I have been that vegan at the potluck, panicking that the omnivores would take too much of the dishes I could actually eat.

We romanticize the starving artist. When we read about George Orwell chewing cloves of garlic to trick his stomach into thinking he'd eaten a meal, van Gogh selling not a single painting in his lifetime except to his own brother, or James Brown growing up in a brothel, we attribute some of their talent to having suffered. While these luminaries certainly exemplify the value of working hard and letting nothing stop them from practicing their art, that's not the lesson we're inclined to learn from these anecdotes. We see how those who have come before us have abandoned their families and ruined their health and sanity in order to produce work of lasting value, and we tend to idolize them for it. We believe there is strength in going without, that we're worth more if we've come from nothing, that there's something inherently noble about laboring in obscurity. The myth of the starving artist is a crock of shit, and yet we always come back for seconds.

Cultural historians agree that the enduring image of the artist starving in a garret originated with Thomas Chatterton, the writer of pseudomedieval poetry who committed suicide in 1770 at the age of seventeen. Henry Wallis's 1856 painting, *The Death of Chatterton,* shows a redheaded man sprawled over threadbare bedclothes, skin tinged blue from the arsenic. The sloping attic walls are filmed in dirt and soot. A lonely geranium sits on the windowsill, the one note of color in this unrelentingly miserable existence. It is a scene of squalor and melodrama, and it utterly seduces us.

We succumb to the false romance of the poet who sacrifices all worldly pleasures for his art, the false purity of the ascetic who whips and starves himself to grow ever closer to God. We give way to either/or thinking and define ourselves by the negative spaces.

With the starving artist trope on one hand and desire for recognition on the other—contrapuntal manifestations of the ego—the result is an irresolvable paradox. How can we *ever* be content with what we have? Content with who we are? Even commercially successful artists sometimes work under a scarcity mentality: *there are only so many artists who can be taken seriously, and I am not one of them.* An artist can make an abundant living and still feel creatively impoverished.

Here's the saddest part: if all along we've been creating from a place of lack, what might we be capable of if we drew from a full well?

I don't know about you, but *I* want to find out.

At the Boston Book Festival in October 2013, I stopped by the Grub Street booth and chose my "literary fortune" out of a glass jar full of buttons. What did I pick?

Starving artist.

"Nope," I said cheerfully to the girl behind the table. "Never again." I dropped the pin back in the jar and chose another. *Enfant terrible.*

I laughed. "Now *that's* more like it."

You must follow the path that opens to you and you must never stop. And it will demand that you shed your skin, over and over and over again. Your skin must be shed for that skin is not the skin of a writer; it is the skin of whatever you were before.

—STEPHEN HARROD BUHNER

WHEN FAILURE
ISN'T FAILURE

Misapprehension #9: *If I give up, then I'm a loser.*

Tenacity is an admirable trait, but much of the time we're tenacious in the wrong way. We cling to the very things we should let go of: past triumphs. Particular outcomes. Other people's yardsticks.

Fresh out of college I got a job as an editorial assistant at a nonfiction imprint at HarperCollins. Each day we received several unsolicited queries in the mail, virtually none of which were worth rescuing from the slush pile. No one seemed to understand the concept of a platform; these were just random people all over the country wanting to write books on topics they were not remotely qualified to write about. My favorite came from a (male) lawyer in Atlanta who sent us a spiral-bound manual of vagina-tightening exercises; at least that one was good for a laugh. Sometimes I wound up writing multiple rejection letters to the same person regarding wildly different projects.

But *I* was an aspiring writer too, revising my first novel on lunch breaks and after six o'clock. How did I know I wasn't similarly delusional?

Augusten Burroughs has a wonderfully bracing chapter in *This Is How: Surviving What You Think You Can't* entitled "How to Hold Onto Your Dream or Maybe Not." He recounts performing a monologue in acting class and being convinced of his brilliance before his teacher gave him a humiliatingly justified reality check. Kris Carr tells a similar story of her "mediocre" acting career before a cancer diagnosis pointed her toward writing her bestselling plant-based *Crazy Sexy Kitchen* cookbooks. Both of these writers had to fail at one thing before they could "hit it big" at something else.

We need to rejig our concepts of "success" and "failure." As Sarah Lewis writes in *The Rise: Creativity, the Gift of Failure, and the Search for Mastery,* surrender means giving over, not giving up.

This is about much more than knowing when to cut your losses though. If we strive for years, putting everything we have into our ambition and still falling short—if something *just isn't going to happen*, be it a six-figure book deal or a slot on *American Idol*—it is very tempting to view this outcome as a tragedy. Hopes are dashed. Our ambition has not been fulfilled. But this so-called failure invariably points the way to something that *is* going to happen, something that *is* meant to be, something that will probably fulfill us in an even more profound way.

But we can't grow into that other destiny if we're holding on to the pipe dream.

Only when we connect our misery to our cravings can we begin to solve our dilemma.

—HILDEGARD OF BINGEN

FACE THE UGLY

Misapprehension #10: *My feelings are always justified.*

People often say, in New Age and self-help circles especially, that "feelings aren't wrong." I get where they're coming from, but that doesn't mean your emotional reactions are always justified. Your feelings may only be "true" in the sense that they are markers, fluorescent road tabs on an unlit highway in the middle of the night, leading you mile by lonely mile to a better place.

If we're not careful, the "feelings aren't wrong" line of thought can tempt us to blame our discontent and disappointment on other people's failings, when we *ought* to take responsibility for what we feel, how we express it, and in what direction it leads us to grow. As the entrepreneur and business coach Marie Forleo says, "Envy is often a clue that there's something latent in you that needs to be expressed." The onus is on *you,* my friend.

You have very little control over how your work is received in the wider world. You do, however, have complete control over your reaction to the world's reaction. You must monitor and interpret your feelings on a continual basis so that they don't turn you into someone you don't want to be. Gayle Forman, the bestselling author of *If I Stay,* had a disappointing experience with her first novel, and wrote about how she decided to react to it: "I understood that if I gave in to the bitterness, it would do what bitterness does, it would corrode me from the inside out, eat away at the soft, open parts of me where I'm pretty sure the stories come from."

Once acquired, it is very difficult to shed a negativity bias, and by definition, once inside you, the bias is invisible. You'll believe every mad, mean thought that comes into your head, and you will be too miserable to keep from blaming anyone else in the vicinity. And as Gayle Forman hints, in the midst of all this turmoil you'll wind up neglecting your art, the thing that brought you here in the first place.

You don't want to be that warped and bitter person, right?

Right. So don't be.

Face your ugly feelings. Write them in your journal, exorcise them with a trusted friend over a bottle of pinot noir, scrawl them on your bathroom mirror with that lipstick you never use. Now you know why you saved it.

*Envy . . . consists in seeing things never in them-
selves, but only in their relations . . . If you desire
glory, you may envy Napoleon, but Napoleon
envied Caesar, Caesar envied Alexander, and
Alexander, I daresay, envied Hercules, who
never existed.*

—BERTRAND RUSSELL

ALL THIS MONEY CAN'T BUY
ME A TIME MACHINE

Misapprehension #11: *I'm way more talented than people who are more successful than I am.*

A few years ago I got to meet my all-time favorite singer-songwriter. I didn't want to gush, but it didn't feel right to hold back either. So I told her just how much her music meant to me, how her earlier albums supplied me with the anthems of my teen years.

She thanked me for being a fan. Then she began to rant about how unfair it was that someone like Katy Perry could be so famous when she doesn't even write her own songs. I wanted to say to her, *Why does it matter that Katy Perry is more famous than you'll ever be? You are insanely talented, you have a devoted fan base, and you are making a living at your art.* Her diatribe felt a little insulting, as if the opinions of millions of anonymous teenyboppers mattered more to her than someone who'd loved her music since the age of thirteen and had been to see her in concert four times.

This sort of envy is understandable—you work hard to

develop your talent, and you want to be rewarded in kind—but it is also bizarre. Would you really prefer to have millions of people passing commentary all over the Internet about the fact that your ex-husband claims you were a mediocre lay? Do you *really* want that for your life? I bet some days even Katy Perry doesn't envy Katy Perry. They say nobody knows as well as celebrities just how insane it is to want to be famous. If the rest of us could experience all the gossip and the stalkers and the lurking oblivion of money and drugs and madness, we wouldn't want it anymore.

When my once-favorite musician came out with something more "poppy"—a song that might actually put her on the charts—it wasn't anywhere near as good as her earlier stuff, back when she wasn't writing or composing to attract an audience. My heart sank as I watched her perform this new song on a morning news show. Our art should grow and evolve over time, of course, but it simply doesn't work if we're striving to be received in a particular way.

I once checked into an Airbnb apartment in Miami Beach, and found a sign propped on the air conditioner that read: BE YOUR OWN KIND OF BEAUTIFUL. Of course, this applies to far more than one's face, figure, or wardrobe. If you keep wanting what *someone else* has, you can't grow into everything *you* could be.

Remember that not getting what you want is sometimes a stroke of good luck.

—H. JACKSON BROWN, JR.

WHAT YOU DESERVE?

Misapprehension #12: *The world is so unfair. Why give me all this talent and ambition but no success?*

A well-known novelist live-tweeted her emotional meltdown when her book didn't make *The New York Times* best-of-year list. "I never complain about this shit," she wrote, "but there are MANY books on that notable list with reviews that were NOWHERE near as good as mine."

Let's look at the mind-set that enables the downward spiral into bitterness and self-pity. When you hinge your perception of success or failure on how your work is received, you create your own misery.

No one's saying it's easy to separate your effort from its reception—it's a process that will likely unfold over a period of years—but until you unplug that connection your sense of worth and well-being will always be at the mercy of forces beyond your control. Your work and the recognition it receives are *completely* separate. If you see the world in terms of what's *yours*, what you *deserve*, what the world *owes* you, then you will never be satisfied with the life that you have. Picture me with a fluorescent-orange megaphone here:

The world owes you nothing.

You may think, "But I *don't* think I'm entitled. I *know* I have to earn it." Yet if you look back over the past ten or twenty or thirty years, at the various ways in which you may have waited for your life to happen to you, you begin to see that this passivity has been an *expectancy*: entitlement in a softer guise.

Just as you must pay your own rent, empty your own trash, and feed and clothe the children you have brought into the world, you must take responsibility for your own creative life. No one is victimizing you. No one is denying you your rightful glory. Indeed, this has nothing to do with anyone else at all, and everything to do with you.

And so we circle back to the dark legacy of capitalism: some people matter, and other people don't. We gauge success not by how we have grown in wisdom and compassion, but by the trappings we've acquired. To have more money than our "friends," a more prestigious job, a bigger house, more exotic vacations: we covet these things, we gloat over these things even if we can't admit to ourselves that we do. So what if you're an artist who believes you're above all this? You think you're exempt?

Of course, we keep up these appearances because we are afraid no one will see us without our frills and finery, that *we* won't matter. We have to ask ourselves: what is the need *underneath* the hunger for recognition? We must answer this question on a fundamental level before we can even get to the nonsense we've told ourselves about our career trajectories.

For instance, I actually get angry when another pedestrian cuts me off on the street as if I am invisible. Every time it happens I have to bite my tongue to keep from telling the back of their heads just how inconsiderate they are. Weird, right? Why do I need this random stranger to recognize my existence? Am I not quite there until they do?

The problem lies not with the random stranger on the street. It doesn't actually matter whether or not that behavior is objectively inconsiderate. The problem lies with me.

Remember Stuart Smalley, Al Franken's satirical character on *Saturday Night Live*? "I'm good enough, I'm smart enough, and doggone it, people like me"? There's a reason why those skits were so effective.

A few years back I spoke with a commercially successful novelist—literally every book she puts out hits *The New York Times* Bestseller List—and if that's an achievement you've secretly harbored for yourself, I'm about to disillusion you. "It doesn't matter how many copies I sell," she said. "It's never enough. They made me change the ending of my new novel to jibe with what they say readers have come to expect from me. I can't even write the way I want to write."

If you are not enough for yourself now, right here—this very second, books unwritten, songs in the silence, blank canvases, and all—then you will *never* be enough.

WARNING: EGO AT WORK

Pay attention to the way your ego might be trying to wriggle itself out of this. *This is stupid*, it might be saying. *I don't need this, this doesn't apply to me, this is a bunch of bullshit.*

Listen to these rationalizations. This *is* your ticker tape.

PART II

Strategies and Inspiration

There isn't a thing to eat down there in the rabbit hole of your bitterness except your own desperate heart.

—CHERYL STRAYED (AS SUGAR)

TIPTOEING TOWARD
OBJECTIVITY

I sold my first novel in March of 2006, and later that year I returned to the town where I'd done my MA to give a lecture. At a house party a night or two later I fell into conversation with one of the students, who was also in her midtwenties. "I just want you to know I'm not impressed," she said.

How was I supposed to respond to that?

Things could have gone either way for us that night, and I had to follow her lead: our dynamic could have been tense or awkward, or we could have developed a rapport, and thankfully we did. We drank red wine, we went out dancing, we talked about books and writing and the messiness of our relationships with men. Looking back on that night, I see my friend was expressing her envy in a relatively healthy way. *I wish I had a book deal too, but it doesn't really matter. I think you're cool.* My new friend understood that jealousy is tantamount to shadowboxing, that there's no satisfaction to be found in it at all.

I have another friend, Elizabeth, who introduced me to The Work of Byron Katie. (It is actually called "The Work.") Every time a judgment or some other unhappy remark crosses my lips, Elizabeth asks me, "Is that true?" Truth be told, it usually isn't, and we've made short work of The Work.

Facing your feelings requires bravery and fortitude. Analyzing each thought as it scrolls across your ticker tape is an exhausting business, but you *have* to do it if you want to feel any lasting sense of peace in this crazy life. And it does get easier with practice.

Several pages back I told you to scrawl your nastiest thoughts on your bathroom mirror with a tube of lipstick. If that's not your style, here are some other things you can try.

ONE

Carry yourself all the way back to the beginning: the very moment you knew you were an artist, that *this* was what you were put here to do. You may remember that moment quite vividly. It happened for me when I looked at the row of paperbacks on the shelf above my desk—Beverly Cleary, Judy Blume, Nancy Drew—and realized that a real person had written every one of them, that someday I could tell my own stories and give pleasure and insight to people I would never meet. I was nine, but I remember.

Pleasure and insight.

I am not yet a bestselling author, but I have given those things to many people; my mother reminds me of this every time she reads my Amazon reviews. I'm doing what I set out to do, and I'm betting that if you break your original desire down to its essence, you'll be able to say the same.

TWO

Take a sheet of paper and a writing implement, preferably red. (I like to use an old-school china marker. There's something extra-specially satis-fying about pressing down hard and then peel-ing off the paper to "sharpen" it.) You will also require a book of matches and access to a fire-place or some other receptacle that is not too near a smoke detector.

Now write down every thought that comes into your head. Every single thought, even if it's paranoid or depraved or utterly, utterly desper-ate. Do not censor yourself in any way. No one else is going to read this.

Here is a partial transcript of what my ticker tape looked like the first time I did this exercise.

I am a much better writer than I could ever be as an artist. I was a mediocre artist. I AM a mediocre artist. My stories (and all the effort and uncertainty of producing them) feel so trivial compared to all the problems and tragedies of THE REAL WORLD. My contributions are super-fluous and shallow and self-indulgent.

NOTHING I EVER MAKE IS GOOD ENOUGH TO GET ME WHAT I WANT.

Fill your page, front and back. If you feel like it, reach for a second and even a third.

When you are finished writing, read over what you have written. Have you actually believed these thoughts? Why? How does believing them serve you? Do you feel ready to let go of all this?

Then, when you feel ready, strike a match. Don't ball it up and throw it in the recycling bin. Don't feed it to the shredder along with last year's MasterCard statements. *You must burn it.*

THREE

Speaking of paranoia: let's try a visualization. You really have to go as over-the-top with this as you possibly can.

Picture yourself on stage in a darkened auditorium. You're completely unprepared for the TED Talk you're about to give to seventy thousand people, oh, *and* you're dressed in the most ill-considered outfit of your childhood. (In my case, this would be the cow costume I wore to the seventh-grade Halloween dance.)

Everyone is laughing at you. All your best friends, or the people you *thought* were your best friends, are in the front row and they are howling the loudest out of anybody. Your parents are there, all your aunts and uncles and cousins and teachers and colleagues are there, and every single person thinks you are utterly ridiculous.

Feel the preposterousness of this scenario. Take a solid minute and let it sink in.

Now reflect on all the times you've inserted your thoughts into other people's heads, and maybe even resented them for it.

People are just humoring me when they say they love my work.

My mother thinks I'm a failure, only she can't ever bring herself to come out and say it.

My partner resents that I'm spending so much time alone making my art when I ought to be earning half our income. She's going to leave me.

As the psychologist Mihaly Csikszentmihalyi points out in *Creativity: The Psychology of Discovery and Invention*, paranoid thoughts leave you with very little energy left to create. If these feelings are acute and you've run out of strategies, find a therapist (or another, more compatible or competent therapist). Do what you have to do.

Imagining yourself into vulnerable-making situations (like the cow costume in a gym full of raging adolescents) can yield a surprising amount of insight: you're stripping away faulty judgments and interpretations, all the chatter along that mental ticker tape, to reveal raw needs and desires underneath. That's how we can use our messiest feelings to recover the reasons we became artists in the first place.

Be happy for those who are happy,
be compassionate toward those who are unhappy,
be delighted for those who are virtuous,
and be indifferent toward the wicked.

—PATANJALI'S *YOGA SUTRAS* (1:33)

YOUR FANCY DIPLOMA
IN A NEW FRAME

When I'm on the train or out on the street, it feels impossible to refrain from automatic judgments about the strangers around me. I sigh at the too-young/too-old mother pushing a stroller with a cigarette in her other hand, ignoring the older child (or children) trailing behind her clamoring for pizza or candy or soda; I wonder about the unfortunate chain of events that led the man reeking of alcohol who begs for change to such a wasted life. I have to catch myself each time I think these disparaging thoughts about other people. Not only is this not who I want to be—I may be "white" and middle class but I don't have to be arrogant and presumptuous on top of it—but I can't possibly know that I wouldn't be making the same choices in someone else's place.

The word "meritocracy" was coined by a British sociologist, but this philosophy is all too deeply ingrained in American culture, giving rise to the preposterous implication that the wealthy are smarter and more industrious and therefore more deserving of their wealth—and conversely, that those who have "fallen through the cracks" could have avoided their sorry fate had they only drawn upon that bottomless well of strength and resilience and common sense that is easily accessible to the rest of us.

No one's going to admit they actually believe any of this—by definition, a person is not aware of his or her complacence—but their actions and attitudes give it away. As the novelist Junot Díaz says, "We all have a blind spot around our privilege, shaped exactly like us."

It makes me squirm when (lovely, well-intentioned) people say, "Four books? Wow, you're accomplished!" How can I take credit for my "achievements" when I had every upper-middle-class advantage? My parents moved to a town with one of the best public school systems in the state. They bought me every book I ever asked for. There was no question that I was going to college. I got a partial scholarship, and my mother and grandfather paid for the rest. I amassed only fifteen thousand dollars' worth of student debt for grad school and was able to pay it off as soon as I sold my first novel. Bless their hearts, my parents even took it for granted that someday I'd make a living as a writer. (That's even more significant than the financial support.)

There were no odds for me to surmount here. Chances are you've enjoyed a fair amount of privilege in your life too, but these are facts your ego would rather not dwell upon. It's so very tempting to believe you've earned your laurels, but that line of thinking only leads to a sense of entitlement—which, in turn, breeds discontent with the life in front of us.

There are many writers in the world who are just as talented as I am—writers who are *more* talented—who may never see their work in print. There are children living in slums and orphanages who, with a modicum of love and encouragement and the gifts of mentorship and resources, might grow up to become painters and musicians and poets. There are adults out there who *could* have grown into those lives had they enjoyed fairer fortune, along with those who became successful against all odds.

We may try to sound humble when we speak of our work and the honors we've accrued, but are we actually cultivating humility? Do we thank the gods each and every morning for the blessings we've been handed, and the lives and careers that have flourished as a result?

I've never had a big break. I've just had tiny cracks in this wall of indifference until finally the wall wasn't there anymore.

—MOLLY CRABAPPLE

MY, WHAT LOVELY
PROBLEMS I HAVE!

When *Petty Magic* went out of print, the last thing I wanted to do was talk or blog about it. I felt embarrassed and ashamed, as if I could have prevented it by doing more on social media or being more assertive with my publicist. I didn't feel that I could speak honestly about my experience for several reasons: because friends' careers seemed to be going well and I didn't want to rain on anyone else's parade; fear of my frankness being perceived as "sour grapes"; or an ego-driven impulse to pretend things were going well for me work-wise so that no one would think of me as a failure.

This was a minor disappointment in the cosmic scheme of things—a writer's career knows peaks and troughs like any other line of work—but I couldn't help thinking of the Cybermen on *Doctor Who*. Right before they blast you into oblivion, they announce in booming robotic monotone, *YOU WILL BE DELETED!*

I laugh when I draw this comparison, because of course I'd much rather be out of print than blasted into oblivion. No matter what happens, I feel blessed to be alive and healthy and doing what I was born to do. I can't stake my happiness on factors beyond my control—like, say, the decision of some anonymous number cruncher in a Manhattan skyscraper. To do so would be the very definition of insanity. If I hadn't had this pinchy, seemingly humiliating, sometimes-frustrating-as-hell experience, I would not be the person I am now, and I like this version of myself better than any I've ever been.

What really matters? I'm alive, I've got working eyes and ears and hands and feet, I'm surrounded by people who love me. I have not been blasted into oblivion by alien robots.

Still you think, *It isn't enough,* and you probably won't believe me when I tell you that it is. So the next time you are feeling lousy about how your career is going, I have two bits of advice for you.

First, read *Man's Search for Meaning* by Viktor Frankl, a psychotherapist who survived the Nazi death camps. He believed and taught that nothing and no one could ever take away his *mental* freedom. Read the passage in which he and his friends, right smack in the middle of Auschwitz, plan (in vivid detail) the dinner party they're going to throw once the war is over and they're back in Vienna. Alien robot obliterators, Nazi overlords: same difference really.

Secondly, I want you to pretend you are a character in a musical. Act like you're Judy Garland (only not the real Judy Garland, just the sort of characters she played). I want you to declare in the most annoyingly cheerful singsongy voice you can muster:

MY, WHAT LOVELY PROBLEMS I HAVE!

It's true, you know. If you're reading this book I believe I can safely assume that you have a roof over your head, a clean and abundant water supply, and food in the refrigerator. In all likelihood no one is trying to murder you and all your friends and neighbors. Your professional struggles are "champagne problems" even if you can't afford a bottle of Veuve Clicquot.

A paranoid tendency is one obstacle to the free deployment of mental energy. The person who suffers from it usually cannot afford to become interested in the world from an objective, impartial viewpoint, and therefore is unable to learn much that is new.

—MIHALY CSIKSZENTMIHALYI

BANDWIDTH AND SNUBBERY

There is a writer I greatly admire who, every time my editor asks if she'll read my forthcoming novel, declines with a series of very good excuses. And every time I see her name on the back cover of someone else's book I can't help thinking, *You had time to read* this *novel, though, didn't you?*

When I start off on this churlish line of thought, I must once again lead myself through a series of incontrovertible facts.

1. If a writer agrees to read and blurb every single manuscript that crosses his desk, he will have no time to work on his own projects.

2. If a writer agrees to read and blurb every single manuscript that crosses his desk, that willingness actually diminishes the value of his praise.

3. It is kind and gracious to support your fellow artists, particularly those who are not as far along in their careers as you are, but this does *not* translate into obligation of any

kind. Put another way, since it bears repeating: nobody owes anybody anything.

I used to feel affronted when someone didn't respond to my e-mail, said no to what I felt was a perfectly reasonable request, or responded with excuses when I made overtures of friendship. I felt disrespected and ignored.

Someone didn't have the energy to give me what I wanted from them at that point in time, so I expended *my* energy feeling resentful about it. You see the absurdity of this, right?

You can think of energy expenditure in terms of bandwidth. Nobody has unlimited bandwidth. None of us has more than twenty-four hours in a day. We all need sleep each night. All of us have projects to complete, existing relationships to nurture, meals to cook, bills to pay. If someone says in not so many words that they don't have time for you, they are not snubbing you. To snub someone is deliberately mean, whereas most rejection isn't personal. In the rare cases when it is—someone you've been chatting with at a cocktail party excuses herself to go to the bathroom, and spends the rest of the evening slinking out of every room you walk into—what that person might think of you has absolutely no bearing on your experience anyhow. When someone says they don't have time to spare, it's most likely that what you're asking of them would exceed their bandwidth.

These days, when someone tells me no, I take a moment to admire that person for politely choosing to maintain their own sanity. Instead of resenting them, I try to emulate them. There are lots and lots of people I can only encourage and support in the most general way, in 140 characters or less.

So if someone isn't responding to you in the way you would like, this is the thing to remind yourself of: it's bandwidth, not snubbery. Notice how acknowledging others' time and energy limitations actually frees up your own.

Behind the cliché that you create your own reality there is a shadow: if you don't create your own reality, it will be created for you.

—DEEPAK CHOPRA

A MERRY HEART DOETH
GOOD LIKE A MEDICINE

Recently I was teasing a friend about her quasi-secret romance by pretending I had no idea what she was obliquely referring to. We were very much enjoying talking *around* the exciting new relationship she wasn't ready to share with the world just yet. "I have discovered the secret to a happy life," I told her. "You must laugh at yourself as often and as uproariously as possible."

People tell me I laugh a lot too, but I don't remember laughing all that much when I was a kid. I'm pretty sure I've grown into a happier person since then. The Germans have one of their terrific compound nouns for the disposition I've been semiconsciously trying to cultivate: *Frohnatur,* a cheerful nature. Have you noticed that when you're in a really good mood, you buoy everyone around you, or if someone you know is smiling and giddy, they buoy you? Putting yourself in a happy frame of mind should be considered a civic duty: not only does it do you zero good to linger on your so-called failures and inadequacies, it doesn't do anybody around you any good either.

My friend David, an actor and singer, faced this issue while serving as manager of his college gospel choir. After the first semester the choir director took him aside and said, "Here's the thing, David: you're a great presence, but your moods somehow *move the room*. If you're upset or angry, or if you're in an attitude, then rehearsals play out like that. And if you're happy, everybody's happy. You need to get it together, because if you're going to keep coming to my rehearsals with these changing moods, then we'll have to find a new manager." David recalled this conversation after I told him how much joy and positive energy he invariably brings to the yoga studio, so I think it's safe to say he learned that lesson!

But how do we learn to center ourselves when life gives us reason to feel angry or upset?

These days the self-help industry is all about gratitude. Life coaches and motivational speakers tell us that counting our blessings will boost (and even out) our moods, that happiness is a state of *being* rather than *having*. On the other hand, if we focus too much on making lists of the things we know we ought to feel grateful for, we might just end up feeling guilty that we don't stop often enough to thank the universe for having hands and ears and eyeballs in fine working order.

So let's make a different kind of list. I want you to think of the times you've been dizzyingly, ecstatically, *out-of-your-mind* happy. Take out a piece of paper and write out everything you can remember. Here, I'll do it too.

1. *My dad had a paper route when my sister and I were kids, and one winter evening he dropped us off at Stokes Hill so we could go sledding while he settled his business accounts. It was seven or eight o'clock, we were the only people there, and I remember trudging back up the snowy hill, taking deep lungfuls of frosty night air and looking up at the stars with my little sister laughing at my side.*

2. *A few years ago my sister and friends and I climbed Machu Picchu—the mountain overlooking the archaeological site, that is—and while I spent more than a few thoughts on the way up feeling annoyed with myself for not keeping in better shape,*

when I finally got to the top I couldn't stop giggling. We were intoxicated by the wind and the sky and the ancient city laid out before us.

3. *Last spring I took an early morning flight from Cork to London to visit my best friend. He said, "Go up and take a nap while I finish your novel." You know how it is when you fall asleep in the bed of someone you love; you feel very safe and comforted. An hour later he opened the bedroom door. "I've finished," he said softly. "Come down and let's talk about it. I'll put the kettle on."*

Interesting, isn't it, how the experiences that have given me the greatest pleasure have little if anything to do with professional recognition? (My writer friend giving me feedback on my manuscript *is* professional in a sense, but we'd be having that conversation even if I had no intention of publishing my work.) The glories of nature, tapping into the magic of the unseen, connecting with friends and family on a meaningful level: these are the experiences that bliss me out.

If you make time every day to create an experience that will give you that warm glow of happiness—even a simple thing like telling your bawdiest joke to someone who hasn't heard it before—you will notice people beginning to comment on your cheerful temperament as if you hadn't been all that happy before, and maybe you weren't, really. But in the all-consuming joy of a moment well lived, you'll remember your blessings down deep in your bones. You won't actually have to count them.

When all your desires are distilled
You will cast just two votes:
To love more,
And be happy.

—HAFIZ

(TRANSLATED BY DANIEL LADINSKY)

BE YOUR OWN MAMA

Something unfortunate happened when I was three years old. It is one of my earliest memories. My parents had taken me over to my aunt's house for a holiday celebration, and at the end of the night they strapped me in my car seat and went back into the house to finish their good-byes. The car was probably no more than twenty feet from the front door, but it might have been a thousand miles for how freaked out I was to be in the cold and dark by myself.

Through the front window I could see my dad and my uncle chatting, the Christmas tree lit up behind them, and I sobbed my little heart out. All this is as clear as if it happened only a handful of years ago (I remember the little plastic cowgirl toy I was holding, and that it fell between the vinyl seats and I never saw it again), but I don't remember how I felt when they came back to the car. I can't recall what it was like to be comforted in that moment. I certainly don't blame my parents for how upset I was that night—they couldn't have left me there for more than a minute or two—but as you can see, I have never quite gotten over it either.

Recently I found myself recounting this story in a conversation about attachment parenting. My friend said, "You need to go back in your mind, take that baby out of the car, and *love* her."

This advice has revolutionized the way I view my creative and personal needs, not to mention the way I respond to my thoughts. You need to do for yourself all that you'd do for your three-year-old self—or your son or daughter, if that's easier to picture. You need to be every bit as loving and accepting of yourself as you would be of a child in your care. When we're consistently too strict and perfectionistic with ourselves, is it any wonder we move through our daily lives with a lingering feeling of inadequacy?

After that conversation with my friend, I started to notice all the seemingly insignificant ways in which I was neglecting myself.

1. If the buttons fell off my daughter's coat, I'd sew them back on right away. (I wouldn't let her go out into the winter cold with her coat hanging open.)

2. My daughter would never run out of clean underpants.

3. If my daughter was feeling cranky and dispirited, I'd put her down for a nap. (I wouldn't make her feel guilty for not being "productive enough.")

4. If my daughter wanted to draw a picture, I would never say, "We don't have time." Even if we were running late, I'd bring crayons and paper for her to use on the train or in the car.

If we take care of our own needs, we won't feel neglected. We won't have to beg someone else to *see* us. When you act like your own mother, you begin to unlearn old patterns of denial, disapproval, and lack. When you are your own mama, approval and enthusiasm are dished out like a warm square meal—not too much, but plenty. When you are your own mama, there is always money for lunch.

If this approach feels a little too woo-woo, consider the principles of Nonviolent Communication, which "focus[es] on clarifying what is being observed, felt, needed, and wanted, rather than on diagnosing and judging." It's very difficult to treat others with compassion if we can't first show it to ourselves.

So instead of responding to your negative ticker tape with: *These are evil thoughts. My friend deserves her success, and I am a terrible person for hating her a little,* take a moment to claim your humanity all over again. Respond to yourself as if you were your child, who's just come home from kindergarten tearfully wishing it were *her* birthday tomorrow instead of her classmate's. Treat yourself to a cookie (or two) and a really good storybook.

Conceit is an iron gate that admits no new knowledge,
no expansive possibilities, nor constructive ideas . . .
Nothing novel or festive ever happens.

—EPICTETUS

(TRANSLATED BY SHARON LEBELL)

WWJCD?

If you've seen *The Power of Myth,* Bill Moyers's 1987 interview series with Joseph Campbell, you know why I fell into deep and abiding grandpa-love with the famous mythologist. You probably did too. He had this wonderfully warm way of interpreting creation, quest, and renewal narratives from various cultures to make them relevant to our own experience, especially our capacity for psychological and spiritual growth. Campbell implies that his famous catchphrase, "Follow your bliss," isn't just a long-term career directive: it's the best way to inhabit the present moment.

Joseph Campbell has also taught me the value of the archetype. An archetype, in the Jungian sense, is a universal image or form dating to the very start of the human experience, and is thus deeply embedded within the collective unconscious. Our earliest ancestors looked to these images to make sense of their individual identities as well as their place in society. By definition, these images will never become obsolete: archetypes are as relevant to you now as they were to our forebears who painted animals on the walls of their caves. As tools for self-exploration, discovery, and invention they are both terrifically useful and terrifically fun.

Here are a few of my favorite archetypes and scriptural figures to get you warmed up.

The Fool

On a trip to the Scottish Highlands, someone snapped a photo of me standing on a peak overlooking a "fairy glen," even more enchanting under a dusting of snow. My back is to the camera and it looks as though I might be about ready to jump off the edge. This picture reminds me of the Fool card in a traditional tarot deck (which is one of the best sources to plumb for archetypes, by the way): I like how free-spirited I come off in that photo even though you can't see my face.

As Alfred Douglas writes in *The Tarot*, the Fool's "lack of experience in the ways of society is seen on the surface to be a disadvantage, but in reality it ensures that his mind is not closed to unusual experiences that are denied to ordinary men." If you truly want to learn, you first have to acknowledge just how little you know. You don't care if people think you're a ninny because you're oblivious to other people's opinions. You want to learn and explore, take advantage of serendipity and grow through your mistakes. Like a court jester or a trickster-god, you point to the truth where others shy from it; like Don Quixote, you'll throw yourself wholeheartedly into seemingly lost causes because you know that nothing good ever came of giving up too soon.

The Mother Goddess

The Museum of Fine Arts in Boston hosts a sketching group every Wednesday night. On one such evening I found myself attracted to a female idol from the Lagunillas culture out of modern-day Mexico. She wore what struck me as a very serene and satisfied expression. I didn't read her label, I just sat down and sketched her using three or four colored pencils.

I finished my drawing, admiring the multicolored effect, and when I finally stood up to read the label I wanted to laugh: *She is ready to assume the role of child bearer.* I want to become a mother someday, but that's only part of why this archetype resonates for me. Indeed, men can draw on this rich archetype just as surely as women can: the focus is on fertility, nurturance, intuition, and renewal, all of which are fundamental elements of the creative process. You might consider the concept of *śakti,* divine creative energy or "unseen potency"— which, as Tracy Pintchman points out in *The Rise of the Goddess in the Hindu Tradition,* the male deity needs the blessing of his female consort in order to access. It makes perfect sense that "psychological androgyny" (a phrase coined by Mihaly Csikszentmihalyi in *Creativity*) should prove a creative advantage, and the goddess archetype encourages that balance of male and female energies.

Inverses of the mother-goddess archetype can be extremely useful as well. Think Kali, the Hindu goddess who eats her own children: on the surface she might be asking you to examine the ways in which you're acting as your own worst enemy, but Hindus also recognize her as the compassionate destroyer of the ego. In this interpretation, the dark goddess devours your attachments and desires, leaving you as vulnerable and full of potential as a newborn.

You might also consider the wicked stepmother, who (as Bruno Bettelheim explains in *The Uses of Enchantment*) serves as a shadow figure through which the child manages his contradictory emotions toward his real-life mother, upon whom he is entirely reliant for his physical and emotional nourishment. Eventually he will be mature enough to handle those contradictions, and the sweet-and-perfect mother and the shadow mother will merge into a mother who is both lovable and complex. What is it you're not quite ready to see?

Hanuman

If you tend to take yourself too seriously, the image of Hanuman the monkey god on your workspace wall might be the perfect antidote. He represents mischief and playfulness, sure, but he also proves himself a loving and devoted friend to Rama and Sita, the hero and heroine of the *Ramayana*. Can you relax and enjoy your work more than you usually have been up 'til now? Can you be a loving and devoted friend when a close colleague reaches a level of success you haven't yet achieved?

When I visited a Hanuman shrine in Bangalore, the priest's apprentice (a small boy) offered me a piece of coconut candy. It was the most delicious thing on a six-week trip already brimming with delicious things. The monkey god reminds me to slow down and savor the sweetest things life has to offer.

The Knight and the Dragon

Around the same time I first watched *The Power of Myth,* my friend Elizabeth gave me some excellent advice. "I know things are challenging for you right now, but you need to pretend you're a knight." The knight doesn't whine that his quest is too difficult, she told me. He doesn't say he's exhausted and his horse is lame and he hasn't had anything to eat but stale crusts of bread for weeks on end, and couldn't the princess at least *try* to save herself instead of sitting around weeping and wringing her hands all day?

The knight doesn't complain. It would never occur to him. He accepts the challenge that is presented to him with grace and stoicism, and gets on with his quest in his kick-ass suit of armor.

Just as fundamental an archetype is the knight's opponent, often a fire-breathing dragon. "Psychologically, the dragon is one's own binding of oneself to one's ego," Campbell explains in one of his interviews with Bill Moyers. "You're captured in your own dragon cage." And as he points out in *The Hero with a Thousand Faces,* the dragon symbolizes the status quo. "A god outgrown becomes immediately a life-destroying demon," he writes. "The form has to be broken and the energies released." So in this sense, the knight can be the costume we put on to confront our limiting beliefs, turning over into wiser, braver versions of ourselves.

The Wise and the Foolish Virgins

The Mansfield Traquair Centre is a deconsecrated church with lovely Renaissance-inspired murals, sometimes referred to as the Sistine Chapel of Edinburgh. Phoebe Anna Traquair's depictions of the Wise and the Foolish Virgins, painted in the 1890s, are particularly pleasing to the eye: the procession of maidens with their Botticelli-esque coifs, half of them carrying ornate casks of oil; then sprawled on the grass, fast asleep, as a magnificent angel with multicolored wings sounds his trumpet; the awe and gratitude of the five haloed Wise Virgins, met by a host of angels at the door to the heavenly banquet.

If you're not familiar with this parable from the book of Matthew, here's a recap. Ten virgins (representing humanity) go out into the night to meet the "bridegroom" (God), who has promised them entry to the kingdom of Heaven. Five are wise, taking extra oil with them to light their lamps should their vigil last longer than anticipated; the other five do not. The bridegroom is delayed, and the girls fall asleep out in the open air. Finally they are awoken and called to receive the bridegroom, but the foolish virgins don't have enough oil left to keep their lamps lit, and the wise virgins proceed to the banquet without them. "Stay alert," the parable concludes, "for you do not know the day or the hour."

The sixteenth-century Spanish mystic St. John of the Cross invokes the story of the Foolish Virgins in this blistering indictment of the human ego:

Some of these beginners, too, make little of their faults, and at other times become over-sad when they see themselves fall into them, thinking themselves to have been saints already; and thus they become angry and impatient with themselves, which is another imperfection. Often they beseech God, with great yearnings, that He will take from them their imperfections and faults, but they do this that they may find themselves at peace, and may not be troubled by them, rather than for God's sake; not realizing that, if He should take their imperfections from them, they would probably become prouder and more presumptuous still. They dislike praising others and love to be praised themselves; sometimes they seek out such praise. Herein they are like the foolish virgins, who, when their lamps could not be lit, sought oil from others.

As St. John implies, the Wise Virgin doesn't expect someone else to correct her mistakes. She exercises common sense, claiming responsibility for her own well-being and encouraging others to do the same, and through these actions she is granted spiritual fulfillment. You know that favored expression of devout ladies of a certain age: "God helps those who help themselves"? We may not be fully prepared for every challenge life throws at us, but if we continually employ the wisdom we've found through experience, we'll be in the best possible shape.

There are, of course, plenty more archetypes where these came from.

- *Refresh your knowledge of the Greek myths.*
- *Practice a form of bibliomancy with the Brothers Grimm, Charles Perrault, or Hans Christian Andersen.*
- *Take a wander through the ancient sculpture galleries of your favorite museum.*
- *Mine the scriptures from the religious tradition of your choice (be it one you grew up in or one you're learning about for the first time).*
- *Flip through a tarot deck and notice which cards, the court cards and major arcana in particular (The Hierophant? The Hanged Man?) prompt some sort of physical reaction, whether energized or squirmy.*

Approach this exercise in a spirit of playfulness, with the expectation only that you will eventually surprise yourself. Look for symbols, colors, patterns. Explore metaphors and allegories. Watch the never-ending cycle of action and consequence playing itself out within a seemingly simple folk or fairy tale, and consider how you might apply "the moral of the story" to whatever's going on in your own life. The elements you feel most drawn to—or unnerved by—will have the most to offer you in the way of self-discovery.

My philosophy is, it's none of my business what people say of me and think of me. I am what I am and I do what I do. I expect nothing and accept everything. And it makes life so much easier.

—ANTHONY HOPKINS

LOVE YOUR FATE, PART 1

If you find yourself between Leicester Square and Covent Garden in London, you may happen upon a pedestrian alleyway called Cecil Court, and there you will find a quaint little print shop called T. Alena Brett. I happened upon this store one melancholy winter afternoon several years ago, and had an eerie feeling about it. I often have this sensation as I'm exploring new places; some wiser part of me—that precocious tendril of consciousness—knows that if I go inside I will find something very useful and inspiring there, something I'm *meant* to have.

The shop was every bit as delightful as it appeared from the street. There were some prints, but much of the inventory consisted of illustrations salvaged out of crumbling old tomes, carefully backed in cardboard and wrapped in cellophane, priced at three or four pounds apiece. As I browsed, the owner gave me a brief history of the premises: Mozart came here to have his hair cut when this place was a barbershop, and in the early twentieth century the space had served as a tearoom. She pointed to the narrow loft area running along the back wall. "There used to be chairs and tables up there," she said.

"Before World War I, Rupert Brooke would come here to write his poems."

I purchased four cardboard-packaged antique illustrations that day, but my favorite came out of *The Brown Fairy Book* by Andrew Lang. The pen-and-ink illustration by Henry Justice Ford shows a sultan on his throne, his retinue behind him and a princess standing at his shoulder. The sultan reacts with consternation to a head on a plate on the tiled floor in front of him, though the princess looks more curious than anything else.

The next time I got online, I Googled the caption—*THE PRINCESS SEES THE MAGIC HEAD*—and when I read the story I got that eerie feeling all over again. The head of a man—alive, talking, but bodiless—follows an elderly seamstress home one day. (It rolls itself along, like a stone, if you are trying to picture this.) Long story short, the head performs a series of miracles for the sultan (sight unseen, that is), and when the sultan offers him anything he desires, he asks, of course, for the princess.

The sultan's daughter looks at the disembodied head and agrees to honor her father's promise. A head on a plate is nobody's idea of a suitable husband, but perhaps the princess has been dipping into the works of Epictetus. She meets her fate with equanimity and is ultimately rewarded for it. (I don't want to spoil the story for you; just look it up on Gutenberg.org, and apologies for the cluelessly racist bits. The ending is worth it. Look it up right now. Go! Read it! I'll wait.)

Here are two things the sultan's daughter has taught me. When you say, "I love and accept my life just as it is," you're not giving up on some other life you should have had instead of this one. You're saying yes to possibilities that, in this moment, you have no way of anticipating.

Secondly, if you want to feel happy and fulfilled, you can't give a single thought to what anyone else might be thinking or whispering about your own situation. Nobody knows what really goes on in that royal bedroom, nor is it anyone's business but hers and his. Happy people live by their own rules.

Be in love with your life
every detail of it

—JACK KEROUAC

LOVE YOUR FATE, PART 2

You are not going to get everything you want, and even when you do, you won't get it precisely when or how you want it. You *know* this, of course, but you secretly expect it anyway. I never saw myself as having a sense of entitlement, but there it is.

When you inevitably don't get what you want, you have two choices: you can accept the facts as they are, or you can rage against the universe. One reaction is sane, and one is not.

So you grudgingly admit that there may be a plan for your life to which you—the conscious, *limited* "you"—do not have access. Here's my favorite example (which I retell from Henry S. Mindlin's essay introducing *The Gift*, Daniel Ladinsky's vibrant translations of Hafiz's poetry). As a very young man the fourteenth-century Sufi poet became wildly infatuated with a girl. She was rich and beautiful, and he was a humble baker's assistant. He composed many gorgeous love poems and grew in notoriety as a poet, but the object of his affection paid him no notice.

Determined against all odds to win the girl's love, Hafiz passed forty nights at the tomb of a certain saint—awake *all night,* mind you—since legend told that anyone devoted enough to complete this vigil would be granted his heart's desire. It's said that at dawn on the fortieth day the archangel Gabriel came to Hafiz and told him he would be given whatever he asked for. Dazzled by the angel's radiance, the young poet forgot all about wanting the girl and asked to know God instead.

Reality, of course, would have been considerably more painful: the rich girl never stopped ignoring the lowly baker's assistant, no doubt marrying someone else. There are several routes the poet's life could have taken from there on out. Hafiz might have spent the rest of his life resenting the woman he did marry for not being the one he actually wanted. He could have played the phony sage, giving hopeful young men shoddy romantic advice over interminable games of Persian chess in smoky back rooms. He could have hardened himself against *all* women, ranting about their faithlessness and sorcery to anyone who would listen.

But Hafiz didn't cry, *WHY DOESN'T SHE WANT ME?* He didn't stew in his bitterness. He opened his heart to God, and more than six centuries later we are still reading his poems.

The only thing that burns in hell is the part of you that won't let go of your life: your memories, your attachments. They burn them all away, but they're not punishing you, they're freeing your soul.

—MEISTER ECKHART
(FOURTEENTH—CENTURY
GERMAN MYSTIC, ATTRIBUTED)

MAKE YOUR OWN ECSTASY

Why do we quote the poetry of Hafiz and Rumi at weddings and yoga retreats? Why are choral groups still rearranging the canticles of Hildegard of Bingen? Why do devout Catholics, art historians, and casual tourists flock to Santa Maria della Vittoria to view *The Ecstasy of St. Teresa*? Each of these art-works offers a glimpse of transcendence, a temporary cause-way from the mundane to the sacred, and they wouldn't be so powerful if we didn't know on some deep level that we can experience those feelings too.

How do you feel at that moment in *The Power of Myth* when Joseph Campbell says to "follow your bliss"? Do you feel ex-cited, maybe scared-in-a-good-way, or are you left with a sink-ing certainty that bliss is something that only happens to other people? That the closest you'll ever come to ecstasy is looking at art made by those who have actually experienced it?

On the contrary, my friend. The word "ecstasy" comes from the Greek, *ek* and *stasis*, "standing outside oneself," and this is what we must do if we are to be granted temporary ac-cess to the divine. In ancient Greece there was a religion much older than the gods and goddesses of Mount Olympus. Plato,

Aristotle, and Pythagoras all took part in these "Eleusinian Mysteries," but they were accessible to everyone.

Those Greek philosophers and their comrades understood that there is nothing passive about bliss. Patanjali says that there are eight limbs of yoga, the *asanas* (or physical) practice being only limb number three. We practice the physical postures, meditation, breathing exercises, compassion for all living things (*ahimsa*), and more so that we may eventually reach the eighth limb, *samadhi*: divine union. We create our own ecstatic experience by cultivating gratitude for all we've been given even as we break through our self-imposed limitations, our outmoded ways of looking at the world and what might lie beyond it. That's what the mystics do when they open themselves to God, and we'd be wise to see them as role models rather than exceptions. They've made their own ecstasy, and so can we.

I've mentioned a few times that I had the great good fortune to attend a writing residency at Hawthornden Castle outside Edinburgh. The month I spent at Hawthornden was the most magical period of my life so far, and I mean that quite literally. While I've always been interested in the supernatural, I hadn't really had any sort of inexplicable experience, and I had come to the conclusion that I was just one of those people weird things *didn't* happen to. I'd spent the night in extremely old places before, including a few castles, but I never felt so much as a cold spot.

Hawthornden changed all that. I didn't have just one mystical experience; I had *an actual series of them*. And if such weird and wonderful things can happen to me—someone to whom weird and wonderful things never happen—then logically that potential must be lying in wait for you too.

I arrived at the castle in a grateful frame of mind, temporarily freed of the financial and emotional pinchiness of home and invigorated by a few days' sightseeing around Edinburgh. As I said, I'd been there before, and each time I returned I felt a stronger sense of belonging.

Every day at Hawthornden I'd go for a walk on the grounds after lunch, usually along a charming circular path that led through the woods, down by the River Esk, and past the caves inside the sandstone cliff on which the castle stands. One afternoon I was lacing up my boots in the mudroom, which also houses a fax machine and other office equipment. I noticed something funny about the YES-brand copy paper. The stack of red-and-white packages atop the filing cabinet lined up like this:

YES

YES

YES

A thought presented itself, as if I hadn't been the one to think it: *This is the answer to a question you haven't asked yet.*

A couple of weeks later I had a particularly productive morning of revisions, and decided to treat myself with a much longer afternoon walk. It had snowed quite heavily the night before, and I traipsed across the fields and lanes and back roads of the surrounding villages with a light heart. I was fizzyingly happy for little apparent reason.

Then something bizarre happened. Thoughts welled up, more of those thoughts that felt as if someone else were thinking them—as if someone were speaking to me inside my head.

As someone who has been writing novels for the past fourteen years, I know pretty well by now how my imagination operates. When you are making things up there is a halt-and-start to it, the *what if* and one or two possibilities followed by another *what if*. This wasn't how my imagination worked at all. It was seamless, fluid, as if someone were there beside me telling a story, and I was silently listening to her speak.

She communicated with the breathless enthusiasm of a child maybe four or five years old. She called me *Mama* and told me we'd been sisters once, a long time ago, when we'd lived with our mother in one of the winding closes of old-town Edinburgh. She told me what her name had been then, and the name she wanted me to give her this time. She even told me something that greatly upset me, something I never would have wished upon myself, and I thought, *There's no way in hell I could be making this up.*

I passed a family of snowpeople in a front yard along the main road leading back to Hawthornden, the man of the house standing at the gate sucking on a cigarette in a discontented fashion, and I felt dizzy at the contrast between the magic happening inside and the world going on as usual all around me.

Crazy people are utterly convinced of their sanity, right? So the fact that I was questioning mine had to be a good sign. "Is this for real?" I said aloud. And then I remembered the copy paper.

Much more happened to me during that month, more than suits our purposes here. The point is that we humans have accustomed ourselves to an *extremely* narrow range of experience. You can dismiss this story as an afternoon reverie, a vivid imagining, or you can be sensible and remember just how little any of us know about anything.

You don't have to spend a month in a Scottish castle to have an ecstatic experience. You need only three things, none of which cost you a cent: time in nature, a diversion from routine, and the intention that something is going to occur that will change you utterly.

Fools pursue desires outside themselves,
Fall into the snares of widespread death:
But wise men, discerning immortality,
Seek not the stable here among unstable things.

—FROM THE KATHA UPANISHAD

HOW TO LET GO

I have a good friend who is a Reiki master. If I'd had any doubts as to the efficacy of "energy healing," they vanished as soon as she laid her hands on my calves. "Part of you still feels like you have to be ready to run at any moment," she said, referring to something unfortunate that happened when I was sixteen (which is more than half my life ago now). "I can feel it in your legs. It's stuck there. It's protecting you, but it's not *serving* you."

I felt my body reacting to what she was saying, as if all my cells were nodding vigorously. You really don't need to hear about the various forms of purging that happened immediately afterward, but suffice it to say the experience was cathartic.

If we don't acknowledge what we feel—if we don't process it in a similar manner to an invoice we receive in the mail—those feelings will take up residence inside us. Your envy and frustration will become part of your fabric of muscle and bone and tendon. You carry your disappointment in your blood. It courses through you and keeps you stuck. And as we've seen, these snarls of energy inside your organs affect everyone around you too.

This right here is where New Age theories and quantum

physics converge. Think of someone worn down by a sad confluence of circumstance, character, and choice. It could be a neighbor who continually allows her family and friends to take advantage of her kindness, a friend always coming down with some mysterious ailment or other that prevents him from having a social life, or someone you sat next to on the train at rush hour, and you didn't even need a good look at his face to know how miserable he was. Think of how these people affect the quality of the air in any room they enter—of how their feelings make *you* feel when you are with them.

We can't do anything about other people's rage and sorrow, but we owe it to ourselves—not to mention our family and colleagues—to deal with *our* shit, to see it and let it go. And if you feel like equanimity is well and truly beyond you, well then: do you see how insidious our limiting beliefs can be?

These stores of stale and unproductive energy accumulate over a lifetime, so the process of releasing them is going to take a while too. You have to be patient with yourself. I want to share with you some of the practices (besides Reiki) that have worked really well for me.

Yoga

When I was in my early twenties I used to go to a yoga studio on Union Street in Park Slope, Brooklyn. I went after work once a week and stuck to the beginners' classes even when my favorite teacher told me to come to the all-levels class. April said, "If we practice yoga every day we can become completely new versions of ourselves. We can be anyone we like." This prospect secretly terrified me to the point that when I moved away to go to grad school I never got around to finding a yoga studio in my new town.

But twelve years later I'm practicing almost every day, so you might say I've grown into April's advice. Flexible bodies make space for mental bendiness, and we're naturally more open to new experiences and new ways of perception.

So find a yoga studio near you, go to a class, and whenever you're tempted to say things like, "I'll never be able to do that," swallow your words and just keep doing your best. Enjoy the practice, keeping in mind that you have no idea what you are actually capable of.

Meditation and Breathwork

This isn't an all-or-nothing proposition: you don't have to get up before sunrise and sit stock-still for an hour every day. You don't need a special pillow. You don't need to chant or visualize anything (although these techniques can be helpful). You don't need a guru. You don't even need a quiet place—you can make a pocket of peace for yourself even on a crowded subway train just by taking deep breaths and keeping your mind as clear as possible.

That said, a quiet place is ideal, and if you sit in a chair or cross-legged on the floor (as opposed to lying down) you're less likely to fall asleep. Try it for five minutes; even the busiest people have five minutes to spare. Breathe deep and slow, cultivating a sweet breath in the pit of your stomach (this may help you to see what I mean by "sweet breath": as you inhale, picture the breath going into your belly and swirling around as if you are stirring a dollop of maple syrup into a bowl of porridge). You are activating your parasympathetic nervous system, and it feels *good*.

Whenever thoughts elbow their way in, gently brush them away again. I like to use the mantra "let go" ("let" on the inhale, "go" on the exhale). Oftentimes my brain keeps buzzing no matter how diligently I try to settle down, but as my yoga teacher Anne says, "If I cannot focus today, at least I can sit here in a joyful way." That said, Patanjali—the big daddy of yoga, as it were—recommends an exhale retention practice as the surest way to calm the mind, and Anne says this exercise has allowed her to relax even when she was beginning to freak out in the middle of a funeral. For example, you can inhale to a count of four, exhale to a count of six, and hold the breath out for a count of eight. (The idea behind exhaling at a higher count is that you're getting rid of stale energy.) This way you're sending oxygen to your cells, too focused on counting your breaths to keep ruminating on whatever was agitating you.

As incredible as it may seem to you now, over time you may grow to crave this daily period of silence.

Mind Mapping and Free Writing

Process-oriented writing exercises are a terrific way to tap into your intuition. Find a big sheet of paper, jot down a pressing question at the center of the page, then write down absolutely every thought that presents itself. Once you've opened this dialogue with your subliminal mind, you'll start touching on the reasons *beneath* your feelings.

Compassionate Eating

More so than any other practice, I credit going vegan with the remarkable creativity, productivity, and contentment I've experienced ever since. Now that I see my life as bigger than me—because my choices affect the animals, the planet, and other people too—I'm far less likely to waste energy thinking petty, envious thoughts.

Maybe forgoing all animal products doesn't feel like a viable lifestyle choice for you right now, and that's okay. Make a start by learning more about veganism, maybe trying "Meatless Mondays" or coconut creamer in your morning coffee, and see how you feel. Becoming more receptive to such dietary possibilities opens us up to positive change in other areas of our lives as well, promoting what Stanford psychologist Carol Dweck calls a "growth mindset" (as opposed to a "fixed mindset," the hallmarks of which are statements starting with *I can't, I'll never, I could never,* and so on).

Try Anything Twice

Reiki, acupuncture, hypnosis, and other alternative therapies can be enormously beneficial provided you actually believe they can help you.

In developing a mindfulness practice we are, in a very real and almost literal sense, reprogramming ourselves for a new life. As Dr. Joe Dispenza writes in *Breaking the Habit of Being Yourself,* "Once we relinquish those [habitual behaviors], we experience an enormous release of energy, and reality magically rearranges itself." Our reality has changed because we finally understand that fulfillment is something we *allow* ourselves, not something we continually have to seek elsewhere.

Sleep that you may wake,
Die that you may live.

—FROM THE PYRAMID TEXTS
OF ANCIENT EGYPT

THE JOLLY GREAT TRUTH

If you go to the church of Santa Maria Novella in Florence, you will find a fresco of the Crucifixion, painted by Masaccio in the early fifteenth century. Hovering above the cross you will see the stereotypically stern and gray-bearded depiction of God the Father and a coffered ceiling beyond an Ionic archway. Christ on his cross is flanked by the Blessed Virgin, St. John, and the Florentine merchants who financed the painting.

This sort of setup, architectural improbability and all, is a euro a dozen in the Renaissance oeuvre; it's the horizontal panel at the bottom of the painting, a crypt scene, that rivets the eye. A skeleton lies on a stone bier beneath an inscription that reads:

IO FUI GIA QUEL CHE VOI SIETE E QUEL
CH' IO SONO VOI ANCOR SARETE.

In other words:

I was once what you are, and what I am, you will also become.

It's human nature, is it not, to require the occasional reminder of what is patently obvious? Even when we pause in our daily goings on, regard our hands or our face in the mirror and think, *Someday I won't inhabit this body anymore, someday this muscle will rot into nothing or my bones will crumple to ash,* we can't quite believe it. We've become rather too attached to our particular pattern of scars and freckles.

Here is a useful corollary to the memento mori. The evolutionary biologist Richard Dawkins has argued vehemently (a little *too* vehemently, perhaps) that any concept of "God" is a delusion, but he has also written about the miracle of any given person's existence. "We are going to die, and that makes us the lucky ones," he writes in *Unweaving the Rainbow.* "Most people are never going to die because they are never going to be born."

If Masaccio's name isn't familiar to you, it's probably because he shuffled off this mortal coil at the age of twenty-six, leaving the fresco at Santa Maria Novella as his de facto masterpiece. When he applied that last daub of paint to the skeleton at the foot of *The Holy Trinity,* could Masaccio have known that we—living on another continent, speaking some other language, nearly six hundred years after his own death—would see his work and take the coldest sort of comfort in its message of inevitability? As the poet Amy McNamara wrote of a departed loved one,

i'm a little less
afraid of the dark
now that you've become part of it.

I have another favorite example of memento mori, also in Florence: the artist Elizabeth Boott Duveneck was laid to rest in the Allori Cemetery in 1888 under a beautiful bronze tomb effigy. My most vivid memory of a 2002 field trip to the Allori is the caretaker showing us a massive and very worn wooden table where corpses were prepared for burial, but I know I must have seen Elizabeth's effigy too. There's a marble copy at the Museum of Fine Arts in Boston, and I make a point to view it every time I go there. The face of the dead woman is rather prim, her collar stiffly Victorian, but you can still feel the love and the grief that went into the carving of this piece, the work of Elizabeth's husband, Frank, along with Clement John Barnhorn. Their friend Henry James wrote of the memorial, "One is touched to tears by this particular example which comes home to one so—of the jolly great truth that it is art alone that triumphs over fate."

Elizabeth is gone and so is Masaccio, but *you* are here. Your eyes are open and your heart is ticking like a metronome inside your chest. Here is the place and now is the time. You won't live forever—and it's very likely your work won't either—but when you look to art for your salvation, like your oldest, dearest friend, it will come through for you every time.

Try not to become a man of success, but rather try to become a man of value. He is considered successful in our day who gets more out of life than he puts in. But a man of value will give more than he receives.

—ALBERT EINSTEIN

MAKE YOURSELF USEFUL

I have two very dear friends who are both brilliant writers.
Deirdre is a special-education teacher who works with severely
autistic children in Dublin. Seanan, after years of volunteer-
ing at a homeless shelter in London on his days off, is now
studying for a degree in social work and interning at a family
services agency in Limerick (which used to have a nickname:
"Stab City." It's been cleaned up a bit but I've no doubt he still
has his work cut out for him).

Both of my friends love and believe in their work wholeheartedly. These aren't "day jobs." I listen to Deirdre talk
about her students, the tenderness she feels for children, *older*
children, who are still wearing diapers, still working out how
to hold a crayon, who will never be able to live on their own—
and I think, *I need to do something this useful.* Aristotle spoke
of *eudaimonia,* the notion that one's personal well-being and
sense of purpose are in society's best interest too, that virtue
is a gift multiplying each time it's given, and my friends live
this philosophy every day of their lives.

Here is the paradox I've been grappling with over the past
few years: art may be almost as necessary as air and water, but

practically speaking, the world doesn't *need* another novel, song, film, or painting. What the world *does* need is more people who go out of their way to be kind to one another. We can express this love through art, but we have to be willing to see it out there without payment or ownership or overt appreciation of any kind, and that's an endeavor most of us over-achievers are willing to leave on the back burner.

It's no coincidence, of course, that Deirdre and Seanan have the healthiest egos of any two writers I have ever met. They give their all to projects they know they may never publish. They would, of course, like their stories to find a wider audience someday, but there is little if any correlation between recognition and fulfillment. Maybe the Irish have a healthier perspective on all this. No one expects to make a full-time living off their writing, so no one flings themselves into a pit of despair when the big book deal doesn't transpire.

My friends have encouraged me by example. Right now I'm just tutoring one day a week at an after-school program, but I have grander ambitions. Funny to think of volunteer work as an "ambition," but these days that's the sort of life I want to live. Everybody and their uncle seems to have a book out these days, or is self-publishing, or is actively aspiring to do either of those things. My "achievements" don't seem to matter like they did before I'd actually achieved them.

I'm not saying you should drop everything right now, run to the nearest soup kitchen, and put on an apron. I'm not saying you should give up on your professional ambitions in favor of the convent. I'm just saying there are a million different ways to find fulfillment *besides* your work, and how many have you tried so far?

Here are some quick and easy ways you can make yourself useful today—soon—pretty much right this second, if you're willing.

1. Acknowledge someone else's usefulness. (Always thank the bus driver.)

2. Listen. (*Actually* listen.) A wise woman once said we have two ears but only one mouth because we're meant to listen twice as often as we speak. When you start seeing everyone you meet as a new teacher rather than someone to be tolerated, sucked up to, or ignored, it's amazing how much you can learn.

3. Smile at strangers. You never know, you might turn somebody's day around, and it's all dominos from there.

These simple actions will probably leave you feeling pretty good about yourself, am I right? Whether you call it *eudaimonia*, good karma, or just acting like a decent human being, everything you put out there *will* come back to you. That's not why you do it, but it's a darn good feeling to carry with you as you move through the world. As the choreographer Twyla Tharp writes in *The Creative Habit,* it's no coincidence if the most generous artists you know also happen to be the *luckiest* artists you know—"and they tend to make others feel lucky to be around them."

So don't try to be enviable. Strive to be useful, and you'll wind up happier *and* more successful.

I am growing jealous of other poets and we will all grow jealous of each other unless we know each other and so feel a share in each other's triumph.

—WILLIAM BUTLER YEATS

CHANGING THE CULTURE

I met a Glasgow writer named Kirsty at Hawthornden, the castle and writing retreat I've mentioned here and there in these pages. Being Scottish and feminist and possessed of a wild and beautiful imagination, Kirsty naturally draws a great deal of inspiration from traditional folk and fairy tales. As a parting gift at the end of our monthlong residency, she made us each a pocket-sized flash fiction zine. At this point, Kirsty had published a slew of short stories and had a practice novel or two under her belt, and her ambition was palpable. (She may have had a touch of wunderkind syndrome, but I'm certainly not throwing any stones.)

The year after Hawthornden, Kirsty got three phenomenal book deals in the UK, US, and Canada. My friend's new publishing house in the U.S. was the very same one that had fired my publisher and eliminated her imprint, then reacted to my contracted second novel—which, by the way, is quite an entertaining and worthwhile book—with a collective yawn. *Shit*, I thought. *I hope they treat Kirsty better than they treated me.*

That was my reaction, but since we're being honest here: it wasn't my *entire* reaction.

I wanted my friend to receive the respect and recognition she deserves, but my mental ticker tape was in half-powered whine mode: *What about MY poor overlooked novel? What about ME?* This situation felt a little like finding out your ex (who dumped *you*, by the way) just asked somebody else to marry him: you can't help feeling a prickle of resentment toward the one he's chosen instead.

A year after that, when an advance reading copy of Kirsty's novel arrived in my mailbox, I thought at first they'd sent me a finished paperback. That was how beautiful and expensively produced this galley was—top-quality papers, deckle edge, embossed title and everything. *They didn't do this for me,* I thought.

This is a completely normal train of thought, but that doesn't mean I want to waste any more time continuing to think it. What does it matter if the editor misspells my name on the cover letter, when the point is Kirsty's novel?

After her book deal, Kirsty and I e-mailed back and forth about the unexpected terror underpinning the fulfillment of one's primary hope and ambition. We wrote about feeling unworthy, suddenly feeling like an impostor. *I really had no idea that you were in a pinchy spot at Hawthornden,* she told me. *In my eyes you were (and are) a success, and had the sort of career I wanted! Funny how we never know quite how things look from the inside.*

Here's the thing: it's in everyone's best interest if we DO share these glimpses of how things really are. No posturing, no putting on a brave face, no pretending we have our shit together when we haven't paid our rent in three months (or are borrowing the rent money from our parents. Guilty as charged). No bullshit between any of us. Just honesty, or at least as much honesty as we are capable of in any given moment.

I told you at the beginning that my sister asks me the tough questions—questions that show me how wise she is even if she can't remember what she said when I refer to it afterward (which is, to my mind, proof that something wonderful is speaking *through* her). I forget the context in this instance, but it doesn't matter. She said, "Why does it always have to be you against the rest of the world?"

Even now, years later, I shiver at how right she was. If you see everyone you meet as either an ally or an adversary, you are going to create a whole lot of unnecessary trouble for yourself. I don't *want* rivals. Rivalry is exhausting, and I need all my energy for my work.

So you have to seek out the people who will *see* you, and let you see them. Maybe you've already got your tribe in place, or maybe you are still assembling it. Either way you must only make friends with people you want to be more like—the folks who, as my friend David says, speak the same language so that words are often unnecessary.

If someone in your circle is stuck in a mind-set of "why hasn't it happened for me?" and "it's not fair," you've got two choices. You can either attempt a heart-to-heart if you think they might listen, or you can cut them loose with your very best wishes. You don't want that negativity rubbing off on you, and you *certainly* don't want to look back on a collection of unfulfilling friendships and realize you've been propagating the negativity yourself. Too often we insulate ourselves with what no longer serves us, or what has *never* served us, so you must choose friends and colleagues who won't hesitate to call you on your nonsense.

And whatever you do, do it mindfully, because you have much more sway than you probably give yourself credit for. *We* create the culture, you know. Each of us has a share in shaping and nurturing this vast and maddening chaos of pattern and color and sound.

And that's the best sort of power, don't you think? So keep making your art even if it feels sometimes like nobody's paying attention. Keep going, keep doing it only because you love it, and every now and again you'll be glad to be proven wrong.

Just be who you are, calm and clear and bright.

—RICHARD BACH

CALM AND CLEAR
AND BRIGHT

We can divide all the world into those who are *Doctor Who* fans and those who have yet to view an episode. If you fall into the latter camp, I highly recommend you watch "Vincent and the Doctor" from season five, which originally aired in 2010. The Doctor takes his companion, Amy Pond, to nineteenth-century Provence to meet Vincent van Gogh, and toward the end of the episode they bring the famous artist on a TARDIS ride into the future.

Amy and the Doctor accompany Vincent to the British National Gallery, where he overhears an art historian telling a tour group that Vincent van Gogh was inarguably one of the greatest artists who ever lived. Vincent stands there in a big room full of the paintings he considered failures, his eyes bright with tears. He is disbelieving and joyful and completely overcome. (I dare you to watch this scene without getting a little misty-eyed yourself.)

They see him home again to the nineteenth century, and Amy wants to hurry back to her own time so she can look at all the paintings in the van Gogh gallery that weren't there before. Surely seeing how successful and acclaimed his art is has changed Vincent's future! Surely he lived a long and happy life knowing his legacy was secure!

But there are no new paintings. Hearing all that glowing praise from a future authority didn't make it any easier for Vincent to live inside his own head.

No one will ever visit you from the future and tell you all that your work means to people who haven't been born yet. (Sad, yes, but I am *probably* correct in making this assertion.) So where does this leave us?

We must grow to become *enough* for ourselves, to fill our own vacancies. We must slay our own demons on our own terms. This may seem like an impossible burden when there is mental illness involved, but you *have* to try. You have to be kind to yourself so that you can keep on making your art; because even if you can't write or paint or compose or dance or act or shoot for your own joy, you'll never know the joy you might deprive others of if you *don't* do it. (Steven Pressfield makes this case most eloquently in the closing pages of *The War of Art*.)

We want to believe that if we weren't already born with an aura of humility and grace and equanimity that we will never know any of those things. We like to sigh that we're creatures of habit, and that's true. It's also the worst kind of cop-out.

Your personality isn't fixed. No one's is. Anyone who says you can't change is just too scared or lazy to strive for it themselves.

So the next time you have a jealous or self-defeating thought, stop and ask yourself:

Is this who I want to be?

You get to make that decision. You absolutely do.

MORE WORDS TO INSPIRE YOU

Illusions: The Adventures of a Reluctant Messiah by Richard Bach

This Is How: Surviving What You Think You Can't by Augusten Burroughs

The Power of Myth, Joseph Campbell's interview series with Bill Moyers (available on DVD)

Creativity: The Psychology of Discovery and Invention by Mihaly Csikszentmihalyi

Breaking the Habit of Being Yourself: How to Lose Your Mind and Create a New One by Joe Dispenza

Mindset: The New Psychology of Success by Carol Dweck

The Art of Living by Epictetus

Man's Search for Meaning by Viktor Frankl

The Gift: Poems by Hafiz, translated by Daniel Ladinsky

The Rise: Creativity, the Gift of Failure, and the Search for Mastery by Sarah Lewis

Show Your Work! 10 Ways to Share Your Creativity and Get Discovered by Austin Kleon

The Yoga Sutras by Patanjali

The War of Art by Steven Pressfield

Tiny Beautiful Things: Advice on Love and Life from Dear Sugar by Cheryl Strayed

The Creative Habit by Twyla Tharp

The Power of Now: A Guide to Spiritual Enlightenment and *A New Earth: Awakening to Your Life's Purpose* by Eckhart Tolle

NOTES

Page

5: **Every ego is a master.** Eckhart Tolle, *A New Earth: Awakening to Your Life's Purpose* (New York: Penguin, 2005), 68.

13: **When Eckhart Tolle was a student in London.** Tolle, *A New Earth*, 30–33.

17: **There has been nothing more empowering.** Jill Bolte Taylor, *My Stroke of Insight: A Brain Scientist's Personal Journey* (New York: Penguin, 2006), 154.

20: **Repetitive, circular rumination.** Timothy D. Wilson, *Redirect: The Surprising New Science of Psychological Change* (New York: Little, Brown, 2011), 58.

25: **A pop star tweets.** "Azealia Banks Sparked a Twitter Fight with Erykah Badu, and Things Got Personal," *Huffington Post*, February 17, 2015, http://www.huffingtonpost.com /2015/02/17/azealia-banks-erykah-badu-twitter_n_6699370 .html.

33: **Let's make sure our ideas of success.** Alain de Botton, "A Kinder, Gentler Philosophy of Success," filmed July 2009, TED video, 16:51, http://www.ted.com/talks/alain_de_botton _a_kinder_gentler_philosophy_of_success.

39: Don't let anyone tell you. Seanan McGuire, Twitter post, November 30, 2014, 8:15 p.m., http://twitter.com /seananmcguire.

44: He was afraid. Dominic Goodall, trans., *Hindu Scriptures* (London: Orion Books, 2005), 48.

45: Necessary arrogance. Eric Maisel, *Staying Sane in the Arts: A Guide for Creative and Performing Artists* (New York: Putnam, 1992), 44.

47: Any sufficiently advanced technology. Arthur C. Clarke, *Profiles of the Future: An Inquiry into the Limits of the Possible*, revised edition (New York: Harper & Row, 1973), 21.

50: I regard consciousness as fundamental. Max Planck, "Interviews with Great Scientists VI," interview by J. W. N. Sullivan, *The Observer*, January 25, 1931.

50: Scientists can't measure the percentage. Michael Gazzaniga, *The Mind's Past* (Berkeley: University of California Press, 1998), 201.

53: There is here no measuring with time. Rainer Maria Rilke, *Letters to a Young Poet*, trans. M. D. Herter Norton (New York: W. W. Norton, 1934), 30.

57: John Richardson's biography of Picasso. Austin Kleon, *Show Your Work! 10 Ways to Share Your Creativity and Get Discovered* (New York: Workman, 2014), 134–136.

58: Picasso had made off with their energy. John Richardson, *A Life of Picasso: The Triumphant Years, 1917–1932* (New York: Knopf, 2007), 454.

59: In his 2008 TED Talk. Benjamin Zander, "The Transformative Power of Classical Music," filmed February 2008, TED video, 20:43, http://www.ted.com/talks/benjamin_zander_on _music_and_passion.

63: "Greatness" is a mental abstraction. Tolle, *A New Earth*, 266.

64: Who's in charge of measuring? Ellen Langer, "Conscious Choice and Mindful Living" (panel discussion, Boston Book Festival, Boston, MA, October 25, 2014).

67: Jim was like a sailor. "Jim Henson's Fantastic World," The Museum of the Moving Image, Queens, NY, 2011.

73: The Consolation. Elizabeth Scot, *Alonzo and Cora, with Other Original Poems* (London: Bunney and Gold, 1801), 123.

79: It is worth wondering. Adam Phillips, *Missing Out: In Praise of the Unlived Life* (New York: Picador, 2012), xv.

85: You must follow the path. Stephen Harrod Buhner, *Ensouling Language: On the Art of Nonfiction and the Writer's Life* (Rochester, VT: Inner Traditions, 2010), 15.

88: Surrender means giving over. Sarah Lewis, *The Rise: Creativity, the Gift of Failure, and the Search for Mastery* (New York: Simon & Schuster, 2014), 86.

89: Only when we connect our misery. Quoted in Avis Clendenen, *Experiencing Hildegard: Jungian Perspectives* (Wilmette, IL: Chiron Publications, 2009), 82.

91: Envy is often a clue. Marie Forleo, "Jealous of People Who 'Have it All'? This May Help," YouTube video, 5:53, posted August 12, 2014, http://www.marieforleo.com/2014/08/jealous -of-others-success/.

92: I understood that if I gave in. Gayle Forman, "Turning Points: Guest Post by Gayle Forman," *Distraction No. 99*, January 11, 2012, http://distraction99.com/2012/01/11/turning-points-guest-post-by-gayle-forman/.

93: Envy . . . consists in seeing things. Bertrand Russell, *The Conquest of Happiness* (New York: The Book League of America, 1930), 71–72.

97: Remember that not getting what you want. H. Jackson Brown, Jr., *The Complete Life's Little Instruction Book: 1,560 Suggestions, Observations, and Reminders on How to Live a Happy and Rewarding Life* (Nashville: Thomas Nelson, 2007), 222.

99: A well-known novelist. "Ayelet Waldman Has No Idea How Non-Notable It Is to Write a Novel," *Gawker*, December 4, 2014, http://review.gawker.com/ayelet-waldman-has-no-idea-how-non-notable-it-is-to-wri-1666698969.

107: There isn't a thing to eat. Cheryl Strayed, "We Are All Savages Inside," *The Rumpus*, March 31, 2011, http://therumpus.net/2011/03/dear-sugar-the-rumpus-advice-column-69-we-are-all-savages-inside/.

115: Paranoid thoughts. Mihaly Csikszentmihali, *Creativity: The Psychology of Discovery and Invention* (New York: HarperCollins, 1996), 345.

117: Be happy for those who are happy. Patanjali, *Yoga Sutras*, trans. Sharon Gannon in *The Jivamukti Chant Book* (New York: Jivamukti Press, 2003), book I, verse 33.

120: We all have a blind spot. Junot Díaz, keynote address, Facing Race conference, November 16, 2012.

123: I've never had a big break. Molly Crabapple, "Molly Crabapple's 15 Rules for Creative Success in the Internet Age," *Boing Boing,* November 4, 2014, http://boingboing.net /2014/11/04/molly-crabapples-rules-for-c.html.

129: A paranoid tendency. Csikszentmihalyi, 345.

135: Behind the cliché. Deepak Chopra, introduction to *Supernormal: Science, Yoga, and the Evidence for Extraordinary Psychic Abilities,* by Dean Radin (New York: Random House, 2013), xi.

138: Here's the thing, David. David Jiles, interview by author, Jamaica Plain, MA, June 21, 2015.

143: When all your desires are distilled. Hafiz, *The Gift,* trans. Daniel Ladinsky (New York: Penguin, 1999), 41.

147: The principles of Nonviolent Communication. "Nonviolent Communication Is . . ." *The Center for Nonviolent Communication,* accessed November 28, 2015, https://www.cnvc .org/Training/NVC-Concepts.

149: Conceit is an iron gate. Epictetus, *The Art of Living: The Classical Manual on Virtue, Happiness, and Effectiveness,* trans. Sharon Lebell (New York: Harper San Francisco, 1994), 87.

152: The Fool's lack of experience. Alfred Douglas, *The Tarot: The Origins, Meaning and Uses of the Cards* (New York: Penguin, 1972), 48.

153: Divine creative energy. Tracy Pintchman, *The Rise of the Goddess in the Hindu Tradition* (Albany: State University of New York Press, 1994), 98.

153: Psychological androgyny. Csikszentmihalyi, 70–71.

154: The wicked stepmother. Bruno Bettelheim, *The Uses of Enchantment: The Meaning and Importance of Fairy Tales* (New York: Vintage Books, 1975), 69.

155: A god outgrown. Joseph Campbell, *The Hero with a Thousand Faces* (New York: Pantheon, 1949), 289.

155: A fire-breathing dragon. Joseph Campbell and Bill Moyers, *The Power of Myth*, PBS documentary, 1988.

157: Some of these beginners. St. John of the Cross, *The Dark Night of the Soul*, trans. E. Allison Peers (New York: Doubleday, 1959), 41–42.

161: My philosophy is. Anthony Hopkins, interview by Sean Macaulay, *The Telegraph*, January 31, 2011, http://www.telegraph.co.uk/culture/film/starsandstories/8286801/Anthony-Hopkins-interview.html.

167: Be in love with your life. Jack Kerouac, *Jack Kerouac: Selected Letters 1940–1956*, edited by Ann Charters (New York: Penguin, 1996), 487.

169: The fourteenth-century Sufi poet. Henry S. Mindlin, introduction to *The Gift* by Hafiz, trans. Daniel Ladinsky (New York: Penguin, 1999), 11–12.

179: Fools pursue desires outside themselves. Goodall, 177.

185: Growth mindset. Carol Dweck, *Mindset: The New Psychology of Success* (New York: Random House, 2006).

186: Once we relinquish. Joe Dispenza, *Breaking the Habit of Being Yourself: How to Lose Your Mind and Create a New One* (New York: Hay House, 2012), 170.

187: Sleep that you may wake. Quoted in Jonathan Cott, *The Search for Omm Sety: Reincarnation and Eternal Love* (New York: Doubleday, 1987), 175.

190: We are going to die. Richard Dawkins, *Unweaving the Rainbow: Science, Delusion and the Appetite for Wonder* (New York: Houghton Mifflin, 1998), 1.

191: I'm a little less afraid of the dark. Amy McNamara, "the same face on a number of people," Scarlet Fox Letterpress reading series, Brooklyn, NY, November 19, 2011.

191: One is touched to tears. *Tomb Effigy of Elizabeth Boott Duveneck* (Boston, MA: Museum of Fine Arts, 1894.) Museum exhibit label.

193: Try not to become a man of success. Albert Einstein, interview by William Miller, *Life*, May 2, 1955, 64.

198: The luckiest artists you know. Twyla Tharp, *The Creative Habit: Learn It and Use It for Life* (New York: Simon & Schuster, 2003), 137.

199: I am growing jealous. *Yeats: The Life and Works of William Butler Yeats*. Literary exhibition, National Library of Ireland, Dublin, 2006.

202: I really had no idea. Kirsty Logan, e-mail message to author, April 23, 2014.

205: Just be who you are. Richard Bach, *Illusions: The Adventures of a Reluctant Messiah* (New York: Dell, 1977), 147.

ACKNOWLEDGMENTS

This book exists because two extraordinary women, Nova Ren Suma and Elizabeth Duvivier, encouraged me to write it. *Life Without Envy* started out as a guest post on Nova's blog, *Distraction No. 99,* in February 2012, and Elizabeth has been working her magic in my life since the first time I attended Squam Art Workshops in June 2011. Thank you both so very much for your friendship and belief in me.

The Writers' Room of Boston is my second home, and I often felt as if the manuscript were writing itself on snowy evenings during the first few months of 2015. I am so very lucky to have found such a warm and inclusive community there. Thank you to Debka Colson, Mary Bonina, Kate Gilbert, Alexander Danner, and all my friends at the Room!

I can't even begin to express my gratitude to Mrs. Drue Heinz, Hamish Robinson, and everyone else at the Hawthornden Castle International Retreat for Writers for giving me one of the most profoundly happy and magical months of my life. Thank you to Mishka in Glasgow, too, for showing me the meaning of the Fool card.

Love and thanks to those friends who lead by example,

and whom I have explicitly mentioned in the text: David Jiles, Kirsty Logan, Seanan McDonnell, and Deirdre Sullivan. I am very grateful to Amy McNamara for letting me quote from her poem "the same face on a number of people," Stephanie Garvin for gently nudging me to read Eckhart Tolle, Jenny Schneider for introducing me to the concept of *Frohnatur,* Dixie Buck for encouraging me to "be my own mama," Jean Kennedy Smith for being a friend, Fiona McQuade, Anne Wichmann, and April Martucci for being such fantastic yoga teachers, and Professor Brian Hatcher at Tufts University for all the Hindu pearls. Amiee Wright, thank you for everything. Carrie Weinstein and Tim DeSutter, I hope you both know how instrumental you have been in helping me grow into the person I want to be. Same goes for my dear teacher Victoria Moran, and Marie Manuchehri.

I am extremely blessed to have so many wonderful and supportive friends in my corner: Kelly Brown, Daniel Bullen, Maggie Ginsberg, Keith Godbout, Miranda Aisling Hynes, Mackenzi Lee, Gail Lowry and Paul Brotchie, Kendall Kulper Toniatti, Sierra Melcher, Tom Melcher, Sarah P. Miller, Brendan O'Brien, Diarmuid O'Brien, Aravinda Seshadri, Ailbhe Slevin and Christian O'Reilly, Joelle Renstrom, Amy Lou Stein, Kathleen Sweeney, Cheryl Liu-Lien Tan, McCormick Templeman, Kelly Turley, Anne Weil, and Olivia White. Shaye Areheart, Megan Newman, and Kathy Huck, thank you for being so warm and wise and generous.

Kate Garrick, what would I do without you? I know I could

still do this, but I never ever want to. (And Barney Karpfinger and Cathy Jaque, I'm so happy to be working with you!) Sara Goodman, you're the best—I'm still pinching myself that we got to work together on this. Many hearts to Alicia Adkins-Clancy, Katie Bassel, Emi Battaglia, Lauren Hougen, and everyone else at St. Martin's Press and Macmillan for all their hard work and enthusiasm.

A loving and encouraging family makes getting started in this line of work a heck of a lot easier. My mother supports me unconditionally, Bill brags about my books to anyone who will listen, and my dad encouraged me to see my life as something bigger than my own wants and needs. My grandparents, aunts, uncles, and cousins always treated me like an artist, even when my literary output consisted of illustrated "short stories" on paper torn from yellow legal pads. Kate and Elliot and Mama Jill and Spencer, thank you for being so awesome.

Most of all, a million thank-yous to the brilliant artists and thinkers whose work I draw upon in *Life Without Envy* (and I mean everyone, not just the "good examples." I've shared those anecdotes in the spirit of *we've all been there*). Each of these smart and creative people has helped me to write the book I most needed to read.